TRYING TO TAKE THE MAT

THE MAKING OF A STATE CHAMP

OR AT LEAST A GOOD MAN

DAN BLANCHARD & BRIAN PREECE

Coach,

I hope you enjoy this book as well. I very much enjoy your Facebook posts about your family and other adventures. I still would like to do a book about you down the road.

Brian
Preece

FOREWORD

I met Dakota's dad, Dan Blanchard when Dan was still just a teenager. Dan came over to my house with John Knapp for a wrestling workout. My wife called him Mr. America with all those muscles. Dan was a pretty good wrestler because he was so athletic and tough. He he was still a bit raw when it came to his technique because he had only been wrestling for two years when I met him.

He had a lot of potential, though, and I thought he could be a state champion someday. And one short year later, after a bunch of workouts, he was a state champion wrestler.

As life never stands still, Dan graduated from high school and moved on with his life. I didn't see him again for a while until I bumped into him on the coaching circuit when he became a coach. When we could, we snuck in a few workouts together in between rounds at tournaments. Eventually, Dan left the wrestling circuit to raise his family.

Once again, I didn't see Dan for a while until one day, I bumped into him while I was picking up some food to eat at a restaurant. Dan was waiting to pick up his food too. He told me he had a seven-year-old boy named Dakota and four daughters, too. I asked him if Dakota was wrestling yet, and he said no. I thought that that was actually a good thing and that he might be wise not to push Dakota into wrestling.

Many times, it's better to wait and let a kid find wrestling on their own, even if it doesn't happen until later in life.

Many years after that chance meeting with Dan, I was delighted to hear that Dakota was now a freshman in high school and joined the wrestling team. I searched him out one day at the Silverback Wrestling Club in Willimantic, Connecticut. After the coach there pointed Dakota out, I went right to him. Dakota had no idea who I was. Regardless, I grabbed Dakota by the wrist and said, "Long time ago, I wrestled with your dad. Now, I will wrestle with you."

Dakota was just a freshman in his first year of wrestling and didn't know much yet. And although he was taller and leaner than his dad had been, I was amazed by his athleticism and toughness. He certainly was his dad's boy. In addition, I couldn't help but notice his fantastic flexibility. At that moment, like when I first met his dad, I knew Dakota had a lot of potential.

Over that spring season, from time to time, I would work out with Dakota. Dakota had told his dad about me, and Dan came down to see me. It was great to see my old friend Dan again. It sure brought back some good memories.

That summer, I held a wrestling camp at my home, and Dan made sure that Dakota participated in it. Once again, I was impressed with Dakota and thought he had a lot of promise. Fast-forwarding a couple of years, Dakota had his sophomore year taken from him by knee surgery and his junior year taken as well from the pandemic. I knew that Dan had kept Dakota home from school to do remote learning and that he certainly wasn't letting Dakota run all around during this pandemic. So, I offered to help by working out with Dakota at my home in my own wrestling room from time to time.

Dakota and Dan began coming to my home regularly, and I watched Dakota get better and better each week. I knew Dakota could become an outstanding wrestler the first time I worked out with him at the Silverback Wrestling Club. But after spending as much time as I was now spending with him, I could now see him realizing that potential. I believe Dakota, who has technically only wrestled one year as a high school freshman, has a good chance of doing what his father did; winning a state championship. And if he falls a bit short, it certainly won't be from a lack of trying. Minimally, in some ways, Dakota has already won because he is using the sport of wrestling to build his character. He uses the sport to become a good man who will continue to make himself and those around him better people.

I can't wait to see what he does next year when the Connecticut wrestling mats open back up…

Shirzad Ahmadi
23X World Champion

INTRODUCTION

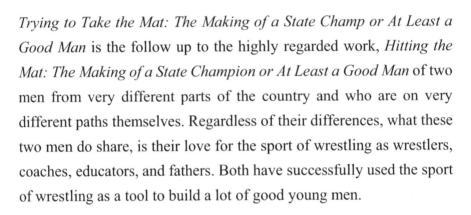

Trying to Take the Mat: The Making of a State Champ or At Least a Good Man is the follow up to the highly regarded work, *Hitting the Mat: The Making of a State Champion or At Least a Good Man* of two men from very different parts of the country and who are on very different paths themselves. Regardless of their differences, what these two men do share, is their love for the sport of wrestling as wrestlers, coaches, educators, and fathers. Both have successfully used the sport of wrestling as a tool to build a lot of good young men.

In this second book, co-author Daniel Blanchard chronicles his son Dakota's frustrating sophomore and junior seasons. As a returning varsity starter coming off a very successful freshman year, Dakota never missed a practice but was repeatedly denied a chance to compete his sophomore year due to a knee injury. Dakota's junior year, a global pandemic threatened to take away a very promising season for the young Dakota who dreams of being a state champ and getting a scholarship to wrestle in college. Eventually, Connecticut's state protocols with COVID-19 does take away his junior year of wrestling.

Meanwhile, co-author Brian Preece explores more aspects of both his coaching days and being a son of a famous wrestling coach in Utah and all the pressure that entailed.

This book will also show how two states from very different parts of the country used different approaches in giving student-athletes opportunities to compete in the 2020-21 school year. Connecticut's philosophy was to stop sports, close schools, wear masks, and social distance. Utah took precautions but kept schools and wrestling mats open for competition.

Furthermore, the readers will experience how the best laid out plans don't always work out. Even in the wrestling world, where we have been taught that hard work is a game-changer and how we need to put our destiny in our own hands, things can go wrong. And no matter what happens on or off the mat, the ability to pick oneself up and carry on is the most essential trait of a wrestler or anyone else trying to become successful. And it's imperative in trying to become a good man.

Good luck next year with your senior season, Dakota!

Barry Davis
4X NCAA Division I All-American
Olympic Silver Medalist
Hall of Famer

ENDORSEMENTS

"Dan and Brian, two great coaches, wrestlers, educators, and maybe even more important, fathers, continue to give us a look inside the real wrestling world of its never-ending ups and downs in their sequel book, *Trying to Take the Mat*. If you want to step inside the wrestling world and gain some insights into building a child into a better adult through a book, this would be the book you want. Or, if you just love the sport of wrestling, you'll love this book, too. Keep up the good work, Dan and Brian, in building good young men through the sport of wrestling."

Dan Gable

"I've always said that the biggest thing in life is the ability to face adversity. This wrestling story of adversity has the makings of something truly great. Like myself, Dakota didn't begin wrestling until the 9th grade. He came out of the gate fast and showed a lot of potential, but unfortunately, he has had one obstacle after another thrown in his way. Life is never perfect. It's often messy and disappointing. And wrestling isn't an exception to that rule. Dan Blanchard and Brian Preece do a great job in this book, sharing their past stories of wrestling and coaching with a steady eye on Dakota's progress in becoming a good man through becoming a great wrestler."

Lee Kemp

4X NCAA Finalist

4X World Cup Champion

Youngest American World Champion Ever

Hall of Famer

"Dan and Brian's unique father-son journey through the sport of wrestling based on Dakota's wrestling career continues in this sequel, *Trying to Take the Mat*. Dakota is older now but faces no fewer challenges. As a matter of fact, times have grown more complex due to injuries and COVID-19. Regardless, Dakota must push on. And his father and coach, Dan, is there to guide him similarly to how Brian's dad was there for him too all those years ago. This book is full of wonderful little stories of coming to age in man's oldest sport and is a must-read for wrestling families."

Ken Chertow

Olympian

"As I read through *Trying to Take the Mat*, it reminded me that successfully picking oneself up and dealing with frustration and disappointments are the things wrestling hands us to build our character. Once again, there are a lot of great wrestlers speaking in the book. And the dual perspectives of Dan Blanchard and Brian Preece continues to be very interesting. Dan, the former champion wrestler rooting for his son, and Brian Preece, who wrestled for his father, one of Utah's greatest coaches, come from very different worlds. But, regardless, they have teamed up to write another great wrestling book. This book opens the door of wrestling for all to come on inside, make oneself comfortable as a dear friend, and root for the wrestlers and their families all over this great nation of ours. I think this book is another wonderful wrestling book created by Brian Preece and Dan Blanchard's synergy. And chances are you will too."

Terry Davis

Author of Vision Quest Book turned Movie

"This is a remarkable story of fathers and sons journeying through the high school wrestling world and weathering the ups and downs that go along with it, such as injuries and even a pandemic. Wrestling saved me and educated me. And now, Dan Blanchard and Brian Preece are using the sport of wrestling to save and then develop our next generation of good young men and women. Go to it, Dan and Brian!"

Mike Foy

5X U.S. National Champion

2X Olympian

Pan-American Gold Medalist

"I know all about overcoming hardship and beating the odds to become a standout wrestler. One has to create opportunities. And that's exactly what Dakota is doing in this book. He fights to find a way to learn and grow among the setbacks of a knee surgery his sophomore year and a pandemic his junior year. Dakota's father and coach, and former standout wrestler, Dan Blanchard, tells a beautiful story of perseverance where we find ourselves rooting for Dakota. And once again, we see Brian Preece complimenting each tale with his wealth of knowledge and experience in coming from the great wrestling state of Utah and being the son of one of its greatest coaches. Pick up this book now. It will inspire you both on and off the mat."

Ben Kjar
UVU's First NCAA DIV I All-American

"Trying to Take the Mat brings another unique lens into the cause and effect of an athlete's journey in the world of high school wrestling. Brian Preece and Dan Blanchard guide you through life's hard-learned lessons of a promising young wrestler and his family. They face one obstacle after another while growing from each one. Brian and Dan come from different worlds of wrestling. And their demographics continue to play a role in how they see wrestling during this tumultuous time in history. Both brilliantly contribute to the wrestling world a can-do attitude through Dakota's ups and downs in his own quest to become a good man through the sport of wrestling."

Katherine Shai
Seven-Time U.S. National Team member

"Dan Blanchard and Brian Preece continue to do a lot of good for this sport with their books based on Dakota's journey through wrestling and young manhood. Every day, Dakota is becoming a better man through wrestling. This book, *Trying to Take the Mat*, makes that very obvious. If you like the sport of wrestling, you are going to love this book."

John Knapp
Head Wrestling Coach
Poway Olympic Regional Training Center

"Trying to take the Mat, helps you see wrestling across this country from different points of view. Whether you are an athlete, coach, or family member, you will have a great inside peek from the back and forth dialogue of Brian Preece and Dan Blanchard. Dan helps you see things from the dad/coach perspective while working with his son, who has tons of promise but hasn't been able to show it yet. With his vast wrestling experiences and knowledge from the son of a coach perspective, Brian deftly compliments and enrichens what Dan is trying to share with the wrestling world. As I shared before with Brian and Dan's previous book, *Hitting the* Mat, coaching your son can sometimes be one of the hardest things someone can do. Learning from both Brian and Dan can help you navigate that challenging process better. I would highly recommend this book to all."

Jeff Newby
Executive Director of USA Wrestling Utah

"The award-winning author Dan Blanchard and Brian Preece have another winner in their next wrestling book, *Trying to Take the Mat*. Their applied knowledge, experience, and insight following the continuing journey of Dakota in the sport of wrestling move one's soul to creating a better world for all. The introspect of the daily grind, the physical and mental demands, and the never-ending failures peppered with some small achievements continue in this book. At times, we feel saddened for Dakota. But we also find ourselves continuously rooting for him and what he and his family are trying to achieve through man's oldest sport. As I mentioned in the first book in this series, *Hitting the Mat*, the wrestling background of both authors, Dan and Brian, makes this is a must-read for wrestlers, parents, and coaches."

Ken Destefanis
National Hall of Fame-CT

"If there were ever a book written about "The Journey," of wrestling, this is it. Dan Blanchard, wrestler, coach, and father of Dakota, takes the reader on an unforgettable adventure with his son through the great sport of wrestling. The good, the bad, the struggle are all here. You can't help but find yourself rooting for both of them. This book is not easy to put down. I was fortunate enough to personally witness much of what Brian Preece expresses in this book as a wrestler and son of one of the greatest coaches in America. He also happens to be one of my best friends. The experiences on and off the mat, in the practice room facing top-level competition, is as insightful and real as it gets. The unbreakable bond between wrestler and coach, father and son, is truly inspiring. An absolute must-read for anyone on "The Journey.""

Ben Ohai
2-Time All American (BYU)
Inductee into the California and Utah Wrestling Hall OF Fame
Inductee into the BYU Athletic Hall of Fame

"Dan Blanchard and his son Dakota's journey through the ups and downs of the wrestling world continues. It's been wonderful to follow this journey through Dan Blanchard's and Brian Preece's sequel, *Trying to Take the Mat.* Like their last book, *Hitting the Mat,* this next book continues to give one an amazing inside peek into the arduous journey of Dakota and the myriad of other wrestlers out there as well. This is another excellent book on developing personal excellence. You should pick it up right now."

John Bennett
World Champ
Hall of Fame

"Dan Blanchard and Brian Preece continue to do exciting things for wrestling in *Trying to Take the Matt.* This sequel book gives another inside peek at the father-son dynamic in this demanding sport of high school wrestling. Through continuing to do hard things like wrestling, sons and fathers become closer and better men. Wrestlers and wrestling families get a copy of this book."

Jack Clark
Executive Director
U.S. Wrestling Foundation

TABLE OF CONTENTS

PART ONE

CHAPTER ONE
EAGER TO TAKE THE MAT

Dan Blanchard: Wow! I can't believe we're back again on the mat for another high school wrestling season. It was one heck of an off-season of wrestling for Dakota. He was invited to wrestle in the Virginia Beach High School Nationals at the 132-pound weight class at the freshmen level. I told his coach I didn't want him sucking weight again by trying to go 126. However, it didn't help much. Dakota must have had a growth spurt because before I knew it, his weight fluctuated between 135-140 pounds, and he was sucking weight anyway.

Thankfully, our regional training site for the Nationals was right down the road from where we live. Dakota wrestled at the Silverback Wrestling Club in Willimantic, Connecticut, five days a week for several months leading up to the Nationals. I was pleased with the level of wrestling and coaching in the Silverback wrestling room.

However, this wrestling experience at Silverback was very different because the coaches locked the wrestling doors to the wrestling room and wouldn't let any parents in the room. We parents had to watch what the kids called the "Sweat Box" workouts through a live video feed that didn't have a good picture and without any audio from another room. I totally understand and appreciate why the Silverback coaches have it set up that way. Still, as a former warrior and life-long learner, I would have preferred to have been in that wrestling room instead.

We are fortunate to have great friends. And I am so grateful for all the people who came forward to donate money to Dakota so he could wrestle in the Nationals. Wrestling on a travel team in the off-season is very expensive. Dakota and I are incredibly grateful to the very generous donations from Peter Albert, Tim Victor, Vic Picone, and Genoveva Person.

Unfortunately, throughout the spring off-season wrestling, Dakota continued to have on and off knee problems. Fortunately, the injury didn't sideline him too much. He wrestled in most of the practices leading up to Nationals and spent many nights icing his knee.

Nationals in Virginia Beach finally came, and I was lucky enough to have a couple of personal days off work. So, I took them, and my wife and I made the ten-hour car ride on a Wednesday night down to Virginia Beach. We got a great deal on the hotel for the first two nights because it was off-season at midweek rates. We arrived at our hotel in the wee hours of the morning on Thursday. And got a few hours of sleep with the sound of the ocean waves in the background.

We had a fabulous room six floors up on the beachside, where we watched a few beautiful sunrises over the next few days. In between wrestling, we took a walk on the beach and wished that the water was a little bit warmer so we could have swum a little bit too. Regardless, there is just something special about walking on the beach in just about any weather conditions.

The Nationals went as I expected. There were a lot of excellent wrestlers there that had way more experience than Dakota. On

Thursday, Dakota got a bye in the first round. In the second round, he ran into a kid from West Virginia who was seeded third in the nation. That kid was awesome. He was beating Dakota 14-2 before he pinned him in the second period. That West Virginia boy would go on to place second in the country. And the fact that Dakota scored upon him and made it all the way to the second period was pretty impressive for my freshman boy, who is still in his first wrestling year.

On the next day, Dakota wrestled again. Dakota hit a beautiful inside leg trip earning him the first takedown of the match. We were pumped! Hooting and hollering! Then the kid hit a switch on Dakota for a two-point reversal. And in a flurry of moves, we saw Dakota make a rookie mistake and drop his head, causing it to be close to his knee. I silently yelled inside my own head, "NO!!!" as his opponent reached for Dakota's head, cradled him, and pinned him.

We Connecticut people were stunned into silence. It all happened so fast. We eventually found our voice again when we complimented Dakota on getting the first takedown and the lesson learned about hanging his head. I also shared with him how the same thing happened to me, too, when I was a freshman wrestling a stud. I could still remember it like it was yesterday. And I never did it again.

That was Dakota's second loss, so he was now out of the tournament. So, my wife Jennifer and I capped the night off by going out for a delicious seafood dinner for just the two of us. We ate at a restaurant on the pier where we spent more money than we should have.

The next day, Saturday, we watched a few hours of wrestling with Dakota. We also bumped into a couple of my old childhood friends

Pat Moynihan and Jeff Oken, whose boys were still wrestling. It was awesome seeing them down there. However, Jenn and I had a long drive home, so we hit the road, and Dakota stayed with the team, as he should have. We reunited back in Connecticut late Sunday night after the boys watched the finals on Sunday and did their own long drive home in the team van.

Summer came, and Dakota kept wrestling at Silverback and traveling to other tournaments within driving distance in the northeastern part of the United States. We also inadvertently added a new wrinkle to Dakota's training of a lot of pool wrestling every time we went to grandma's house. Dakota just couldn't help himself. He had caught the wrestling bug, and now every time he was in grandma's pool, he had to wrestle someone. His ears seemed deaf to his sisters' pleas that they didn't want to wrestle him, so I found myself often doing the hand-to-hand pool combat with him instead so his sisters could flee.

He's become strong and tough. And the pool seems to be gentle on his knee. However, during these hand-fighting sessions, I was continuously reminded how much I need to get back on a regular exercise routine. I was actually sweating in the pool, trying to keep Dakota from dunking me.

As time keeps ticking, fall arrived after summer, just like it always does. And I found myself one night out with John Knapp of KT KIDZ again. You may remember that John is one of my old childhood friends and Junior Olympian teammates. John introduced wrestling to Dakota last fall at his wrestling club in Rocky Hill. During the time we spent together that night, John told me to bring Dakota back down to the club for more workouts. I was pumped. I knew getting in some fall practices again with John Knapp at KT KIDZ would help Dakota have a fantastic sophomore year.

Sadly, once again, things don't always work out the way one hopes they will. Right from the start, Dakota's knee was bothering the heck out of him. By the second week, we figured his knee problems weren't going away, and there was something very wrong. The doctor agreed with us after looking at an MRI. Dakota had torn his meniscus in his right knee in three places, which was causing it to bend in half and flipping over. His knee required immediate surgery.

Dang! His fall season with my old buddy John Knapp was cut short before it could even start. Our dreams of him learning a bunch more over the fall and kicking a bunch more butt because of it over the winter high school season were dashed. And even worse, we then found out that he might also miss his winter high school season. How frustrating… Life is never easy… It rarely goes the way one plans… Every one of us has some kind of cross to carry… But, when considering the long game, that's what builds character, right? That's what builds appreciation for what we do have, right? And that's what makes young boys into good young men, right?

While wearing a brace and going to physical therapy a couple of times a week, Dakota was biting at the bit for the winter wrestling high school season to start. Because of his good physical therapy progress, his doctor dropped him down to one time a week and has cleared him for some light drilling with the team to see how his knee feels.

The first day of the wrestling season finally arrived, and so did Connecticut's first snowstorm. School and wrestling were canceled.

The second day of wrestling season came right after that, and so did Connecticut's second snowstorm. School and wrestling were canceled again. This delay was driving Dakota crazy. He wanted to get on that wrestling mat and test out his knee.

On Wednesday, the snowstorms stopped, and the schools and wrestling mats around Connecticut opened back up. Dakota was pumped to finally be back on the mat, even if it was only light drilling. Dakota's coaches, Coach Torres and Coach Rogers were happy to see Dakota again. They have high expectations for their sophomore wrestler this season.

About twenty minutes into practice, in walked the newest addition to the coaching staff, Dakota's Dad. Me! That's right. After all these years, I'm back on the mat. And I'm pretty excited about helping Dakota, and his team become the best wrestlers and young men they possibly can be. I laced up my wrestling shoes and jumped into a circle run already on with the young wrestlers. My replaced hip was feeling very weak, but I continued nonetheless. We then did some stance and motion, some sprawling, some technique, and some live wrestling. Neither Dakota nor I participated. Both Dakota and I circulate the mat and offer advice to wrestlers when we found opportunities to do so.

What a great practice, even though Dakota and I didn't live wrestle!

On the short ride home in the car, though, Dakota tells me that he thinks he hurt his knee sprawling. He pulls his sweatpants leg up at home, and I see what looks like a new injury. The side of his knee has a bump on it. Dang…

Over the next few days, I'm still pumped to be back on the mat and sharing my knowledge and skills with the wrestling team. And believe it or not, now that I'm back on the wrestling circuit, I was offered three different wrestling coach jobs this year. However, there was never any doubt in my mind of where I'd end up. I'm happy about being on the mat with my son, but I'm also concerned about him. I can see that he is in some discomfort, even though he is taking it easy. And I can also see that he's trying to hide it.

The first Saturday of the season arrives, and just like last year, our team goes to Windham High School for another great workout. Dakota comes home wincing. Now the back of his knee hurts, and so does his calf. I'm worried.

Week two comes, and the running and calisthenics are a little bit better for me, but things don't get better for Dakota. He's not just dealing with his meniscus and the bump on the side of his knee anymore. Now he also has pain in the back of his knee, his calf, his tailbone, his Achilles, and elbow. And he hasn't even wrestled live yet because he's on doctor's orders for only light duty. Then the news gets even worse. Dakota's physical therapist says Dakota's progress has stopped. And now his knee is getting worse instead of better. A frustrated Coach Torres benches Dakota. Physical therapy goes back up to twice a week again.

And Dakota has been sidelined once again. Hmm... We're all frustrated and wondering what's going to happen next…

Brian Preece: By the way, just as a review, or to those that haven't read our first book ("Hitting the Mat: The Making of a State Champion or At Least a Good Man") YET, Daniel is a former 2X state champion wrestler and coach in Connecticut who just began his father-son wrestling journey with his boy Dakota, who decided to start wrestling in his freshman year. I'm the son of a famous Utah wrestling coach. I didn't always like wrestling. Maybe I started the sport too early. But, I eventually found a love of the sport and became a (somewhat) successful high school coach myself.

Daniel has dutifully kept a blog of his and his son's wrestling journey. As I read them, it brings up floods of memories either from my coaching days or my days as a competitor. Through our mutual friend Scott Schulte, who both lived in Connecticut and Utah, Daniel and I came together to do a set of books based on Daniel's blogs that will hopefully enlighten people on the father-son coaching journey, which can be both challenging but hopefully very rewarding. We hope to share the good and the bad of it all in an honest accounting.

My father, who won nine state championships in 12 years of coaching at Uintah High School in a small rural town in eastern Utah (Vernal), coached me in my junior and senior years in high school. However, it would not be at Uintah High School as he resigned from his position as I was going into sixth grade. We would move to the Salt Lake Valley, and I would attend a high school in an affluent area of the valley called Skyline High School. I was actually coached by Alan Albright during my sophomore year. Coach Albright was a former Oklahoma State All-American (who then transferred to BYU bringing him to the Beehive State). He also later coached me at Brigham Young University (BYU) for a season.

As I read Daniel's writings for this week, it brought me back to my sophomore year. In high school, I only missed one practice as a competitor. It was likely that I had a kidney infection of sorts, and it was between our region (league) meet and the state tournament. I still went to practice, and we actually drove out to another school to practice with their team. This was sometimes a common practice for schools in Utah, especially if you didn't have many wrestlers who qualified for state. Sometimes you would group with another school (or two) and have workouts. This way, there was an increased chance of having different workout partners that might be closer to your weight. However, this wasn't really an issue here.

Both of our teams qualified a decent number of wrestlers for the state tournament. We actually qualified eight on our small team of nine wrestlers to the state meet. In contrast, Viewmont, the school we worked out with, qualified pretty much their entire team and had plenty of JV wrestlers as well. In the end, they would place second in the state, and we would place fourth. At that time, Viewmont was coached by Steve Sanderson, the father of Cody, Cole, Cael, and Cyler Sanderson. These names are familiar with wrestlers everywhere. I'm sure, especially that third brother who now is the head coach at Penn State and who won four NCAA championships as a competitor while going undefeated in college and winning an Olympic gold medal. Father Steve is a legendary coach in Utah and was just beginning his coaching career when I was in high school. After a short stint at Viewmont, he would move on to Wasatch High School, where he would win several state championships. He turned that high school program into not just a state powerhouse but a program that was often nationally ranked.

Going over to Viewmont allowed our coach (Alan Albright) a chance to hang out with Steve, as both were college teammates at BYU. But since we had a small squad, it was nice I suppose to have a variety of workout partners. Personally, I wouldn't be able to take advantage of that as I spent the weekend "pissing blood," as they say, though I was feeling a bit better by Monday. The state tournament was Thursday, but no chances were taken, and I sat out practice and observed.

As a sophomore, I had a losing record. I think I was about 12-15 when I entered the state meet. I did manage to place fourth at our region meet, which got me into the state tournament. It was a rough year for me. In junior high (grades 7-9 for me), I had done well. I had placed second in our school district's championship, my eighth and ninth-grade years and won the title in my seventh-grade year. But my interest in wrestling was waning, I hit a growth spurt, wasn't really naturally athletic, and my sophomore year was a struggle. Like many sophomores or younger wrestlers, I was beginning to get a bit better as the season progressed. My big goal was to place at state, but I'm sure my coach (and my Dad) was just hoping I could maybe win a match.

At that time, we had four regions or leagues that made up the 4A (the largest classification at that time. By the way, Utah now has six classifications--I know, way too many). So the top four wrestlers from these region tournaments would qualify for the state meet. Our state used a "formula system," which just meant as a fourth-place wrestler, one would wrestle a region champion from another league. There was no seeding, and as one might expect, some regions were better than others. Our region had a decent reputation but wasn't considered the toughest league. The toughest was from the southern part of Salt Lake Valley who had Brighton High School. They were the dominant large-school program during the late 1970s through the 1980s. But in the end, our league would produce the third and fourth place teams at state and another team placed in the top ten. And our region did have three of the twelve state champions.

I remember at that practice sitting on a bench watching intently a wrestler named Chris Hansen. He was a senior and the wrestler I was going to compete against in the first match of the state meet. He was a 2X state placer and had a dangerous Granby (or Petersen) roll, as all of Steve Sanderson coached wrestlers it seemed. I personally thought he was best on the mat versus on his feet. But I remember Coach Albright telling me to watch him in practice, and I did. It wasn't comforting. I knew he was a good wrestler. The year before, he beat our region champion David Vialpando for third place at the state tournament.

However, as fate turned out, Vialpando was suffering from his own kidney infection that didn't get better. He would withdraw from the state tournament. This meant I would move up on the bracket as our third place wrestler, and our league's fifth-place wrestler would now step into my place and now wrestle Hansen. I would wrestle the second place wrestler from Hansen's region, a wrestler from Woods Cross, who came in with a 28-4 record and was ranked in the top six in the unofficial state rankings.

I didn't find out that I was to be moved up on the bracket until the state tournament's weigh-in. For those that read the last book, I talked about David Vialpando as perhaps being my Dad's favorite wrestler he ever coached. After coaching at Uintah High School, my Dad coached at Cyprus High School for four years, and his last year there, he coached Vialpando. But my Dad quit teaching and coaching altogether as I went into my sophomore year.

Naturally, David and I were friends, and still are, so him not being at the state that year was bittersweet for me. My Dad was sad to not see David have a chance to compete as I was, but at the time, it improved my position a bit on the bracket. Instead of wrestling Hansen, considered the favorite to win the weight class, I got an easier match against a ranked foe. And I took advantage of this new opportunity and scored a big upset win. I don't even remember the score, but I won by three or four points.

Now in the quarterfinals, I actually went up against Todd Norton, my childhood wrestling nemesis who I had wrestled probably two dozen times over the years, never winning. And let's just say the streak continued, and Todd pinned me in the second round. That sent me to the consolation bracket where I picked up a victory against a wrestler from Hillcrest High School, coached by Don Neff, a Hall of Fame wrestling coach and official. Neff and my Dad actually attended Colorado State College (now the University of Northern Colorado). Neff was on the wrestling team and would have been an All-American, but he got injured and missed weight on the last day. Neff was two years younger than my father. My Dad really enjoyed going to the wrestling meets where Neff was the star wrestler with his fraternity brothers, and this is where he really started to love wrestling. Neff was the Brighton dynasty architect, but like my father, resigned amid their winning ways to take jobs at different high schools. Now Neff was turning Hillcrest into a dominant program. I pulled off another victory by three or four points. I think my Dad was pleased that I beat one of Neff's wrestlers, as they were friends and rivals.

Now I had to win a match against one of our region rivals, a wrestler from Granite High School. He beat me in the region for third place, and he beat me again and knocked me out of the tournament. I still feel bad about it because if I had won that match, we would have placed third in the state instead of fourth, though I probably won two more matches than perhaps Coach Albright and my own Dad expected. As I said, it was a rough year. With missing a practice right before state and me still being a bit under the weather, I gave no indication I would do anything positive for the team at state. Ironically, if I had won that last match, I would have wrestled Hansen in the consolation semifinals.

Hansen was actually upset in the semifinals by our region's second-place wrestler, Granger High's Richard Littlewood. Littlewood was pinned by Vialpando but was then moved up to the region champion position when Vialpando had to withdraw. But my good friend in the weight, my old nemesis Todd Norton, beat Littlewood and won the title. His school Brighton also won the team title, Viewmont placed second, Granite was third, and we (Skyline) placed fourth. Though we had a small squad and had a hard time winning a dual meet, often forfeiting three or four weights when there were only 12 weight classes at this time, we placed fourth. Coach Albright thought we could actually win it all, but two of our best wrestlers were upset in the semifinals. We crowned two state champs, the wrestlers who lost in the semifinals came back and placed third, and then I won my two matches. Unfortunately, our other three qualifiers didn't win any matches. Instead of battling for a trophy, we were battling to make the top five after the semifinals.

Legendary BYU coach Fred Davis was contemplating retirement. Coach Albright was considered a strong possibility as his replacement. And my Dad's close friend Ben Ohai, who was coaching at a high school in Utah County, was too. Albright took an assistant coaching job at BYU, then he became the head coach at Spanish Fork. At the same time, Ohai became the assistant coach at BYU, basically swapping coaching positions. Spanish Fork won the 3A state title when I was a senior with my old coach at the helm. Then Davis retired, and Albright was named the next BYU coach, and I would walk on and wrestle for my old high school coach.

Though we had taken fourth in the state and had one returning state champion and four returning state qualifiers, that was pretty much all we had returning. We had no JV team to speak of, and nobody really in the school as a teacher that wanted to be the next wrestling coach. So my Dad stepped up to be the wrestling coach for my next two years at the high school. But I was sad to see Coach Albright leave. I really liked him, but Skyline was never really a wrestling high school. We did produce some top individuals here or there, including the Robbins brothers.

My younger brother Scott would also win a state title. I wrestled with John Robbins in high school. He was 2X state champion and All-American. His oldest brother Greg was the first Utah wrestler to compete at Iowa for Dan Gable and was a medalist in the Pan-American games. I didn't understand at the time why Coach Albright would leave us nor why my Dad left Uintah High School. But as I got older and became a teacher and coach myself, I understood their motivations a bit more. Coaches are always looking for better opportunities or new challenges. Maybe the circumstances where they taught and coached weren't the greatest.

I knew my Dad was a great coach, but our dynamic as coach-father-son was far from perfect. And now, instead of being the gangly 105-pounder that even my own coach and my father hoped might win a match at state, I was thrust into being one of the team leaders. Expectations for me would be higher, and I think Dakota will have that same experience because of his successes.

CHAPTER TWO

IT ISN'T EASY BEING A WRESTLING COACH

AND THAT'S JUST THE PAPERWORK

Dan Blanchard: Well, here we are in week three of Dakota's sophomore wrestling season of high school, and it has been riddled with ups and downs already. One of the cool things about this wrestling season so far is that Tony, the front door security guy, no longer asks me to sign-in because I'm now one of the coaches. Tony is also a former state champ wrestler.

Let me tell you that coaching has changed over the years. When I coached New Britain twenty years ago, it was common for volunteers and old wrestlers to just casually show up and help out. The more bodies in the room, the better. Kids learned a lot from former wrestlers who stopped down once in a while to roll around with them.

However, in today's times, one can't just stop down, roll around, and show some moves anymore. You have to be a certified coach to be on the mat with the kids. Now, I'm not saying if that's good or bad. But, I am saying that it is different, making it a lot harder for a coach to get some extra help. The pool of people shrinks when you have to go online to take a long concussion course with certification. Then, First Aid and CPR certifications, too. Also, add in a very long coaching course. Then they also get fingerprinted and have a lengthy background check. All of these things take a lot of time and cost lots of money. I can't even keep straight anymore how much paperwork I've had to fill out for all of this...

Not many people are going to want to go through this much stuff to help out, especially if they are just a volunteer coach who doesn't get paid. However, with that said, I think my son Dakota knows how much I would give and sacrifice to see him and his team do well. So I do it without complaint because that's what good men and good fathers do. But, again, it seems like the process makes it difficult to volunteer.

Speaking of going through a lot, we almost lost our heavyweight this week after a small scare. Fortunately, we got to keep him, so now we don't have to forfeit that weight class. However, we didn't get so lucky with our lightweight 106-pounder. He is tiny, weighing only 76-pounds. I tried to talk to him and help him understand that he was going to have to pay his dues for a few years. If he hung in there like a real champ, he could be our 106-pound state champ as an upperclassman in a few years. We even tried to recruit another small kid to workout with him. We figured the two of them could have some great upperclassmen years as lightweights. But, I guess we weren't convincing enough because neither kid has shown up to wrestling this week.

We also have a real dilemma with where Dakota will wrestle for the second half of the season when he comes back from his injury. On Monday, Dakota weighed 142-pounds and said that he wanted to wrestle in the 138-pound weight class. The problem is that our senior captain weighs the same weight, too. No one wants Dakota and our senior captain to be in the same weight class…

I tell Dakota that maybe he should consider the 145-pound weight class. I'll get him into the gym to lift some weights and help him gain a little more strength, and he'll probably be okay. Dakota's other coaches disagree and want him to go down to the 132-pound weight class to wrestle. We have a hole in the lineup at 132. And that's where they believe Dakota will have his best chances of helping the team. I'm not sure if Dakota's skinfold fat test will even allow him to go down that low in body weight. He's pretty lean. I guess we'll just have to wait to see what happens…

Wednesday finally arrives, and so does our first wrestling meet of the season. Everybody is fully pumped except for Dakota and me. Dakota is excited for his teammates and loves the feel of team competition. Still, he's bumming it that he can't participate and has to just watch from a distance because of his injury. I too don't participate because I woke up sick and stayed home from work and wrestling. Dang…

Neither Dakota nor I wanted to miss the first wrestling meet of the season, especially against New Britain. I work in the New Britain school district as a teacher. I also used to coach their wrestling team many years ago when volunteers and wrestlers could just walk right into the wrestling room for a workout. They did all the time… It would have been really cool for Dakota to be healthy and wrestling against his dad's old team. It would have been neat for me to be healthy and coach my son and his teammates against my former team on the opening night. But I guess it wasn't meant to be. Maybe next year…

However, something good did come out of Wednesday night. Dakota's weight certification was done. And they said that he can indeed wrestle the 132-pound weight class in January when it becomes the 134-pound weight class due to a growth allowance. Dakota is going to have to be extremely disciplined to pull this off, though. But at least, we now know where he's going to wrestle when he gets released by his doctor.

Also, one of my former student-athletes, Zachary Searle, from the old days when I coached New Britain, introduced himself to Dakota. He said he was compelled to reach out to Dakota. Zachary said Dakota's dad is one of the best men that he knows. Zachary is now a mixed martial arts fighter. He's tough as nails, a great fighter, and a good man.

When Dakota told me about his encounter, I complimented Zachary. I also asked Dakota if he saw the New Britain assistant wrestling coach, Shane Day. After he confirmed that he had, I told him that Shane's dad, the late, great, Jim Day was one of the best men I have ever known... he taught me so much... I'll never forget Coach Day...

Over all these years since Coach Day coached me, I have been paying his good deeds forward to many other young men like Zachary Searle. And in return, guys like Zachary are paying it forward to many other young promising men like my own son, Dakota.

Now back to Dakota's weight. Last year, I shared with all of you in one of my early blogs how Dakota was the freshman 126-pound varsity starter and how 35-years earlier, his dad, me, had held that exact position. Pretty cool, huh? Well, guess what? This year, it looks like Dakota is the 132-pound sophomore varsity starter, and that's also the same exact spot I held 35 years ago once again.

Also, the captain of my team all those years ago was Paul Gilbert, the 138-pound senior. I learned a lot from wrestling with Paul every day in practice. And I'm sure Dakota will learn a lot from wrestling his 138-pound senior captain every day in practice too when he finally does get back on the mat.

Well, it looks like, once again, Dakota is following in my footsteps. So, I had to let him know that I placed fifth in the State that sophomore year of mine, and I'm anticipating that he may do the same or even better. The corners of Dakota's mouth raised upward in a smile as said that he'll do even better. I smiled, too, and said that I hope so and that I'd really love to see him one-up me...

Friday was Dakota's physical therapy session before wrestling practice. On my drive to practice, I got a phone call from my wife to give me the PT report. She said that Jonathan, the physical therapist, says that something weird is going on with Dakota's knee that shouldn't be happening. Uhh... More bad news that I have to break to head coach Torres. Maybe Dakota won't be coming back in early to mid-January...

Well, at least Saturday morning was pretty cool. After all these years, I found myself once again on a team wrestling bus headed out to a day of combat. I had spent many years as an athlete on buses like this. And then a whole bunch of years as a coach on buses like this, too. And now I'm back, this time as a father-coach. And with the other two coaches, we're leading a group of young warriors into battle. I love it!

However, head coach Jon Torres is frustrated, though. We're missing a bunch of kids and will have to give up several forfeits today. Jon laments that the normal kid today is soft and not committed. We only have 11 kids on the bus… I get goosebumps running up and down my spine as I'm looking at those 11 kids. I answer Coach Torres that not everyone has the raw courage of these 11 kids who dare to dream of greatness by stepping onto a wrestling mat.

Coach Torres reminisces about his former coach, the great Coach Crudden. He recalls a time when they were heavily outnumbered. Crudden gave them the speech about King Leonidas, who led 300 Spartans into battle against the Persian "God-King" Xerxes and his invading army of more than 300,000 soldiers. The Spartans bravely held the narrow passage with everything they had in the Battle of Thermopylae. Coach Crudden said to Jon Torres' team, "We'll go with what we have." Coach Torres, scanning the sparsely populated bus, said, "We'll go with what we have," like a true warrior-leader. Assistant wrestling coach, Scot Rogers, who also had Crudden as a coach, shook his head up and down.

At the tournament, I see some of my old friends from the wrestling community. I spent some time talking to Derek Dion, the Southington Coach. Derek always has a great team. As we're talking, he says he doesn't even care about all the wins; he cares about creating good young respectable men. Derek shares with me that every season he gives the team the Douchebag Speech. In it, he instructs his wrestlers how to conduct themselves in a mature good sportsman way at all times, and especially after a painful loss.

I look at Derek and think… no wonder why we're friends. He's my type of guy—a good man who builds up other good men by doing something hard, like wrestling.

The tournament went well. The team wrestled awesome in some places and made costly mistakes in others. We put two guys in the finals, had a few that just missed the semi-finals, and a bunch of new kids that wrestled hard and showed some promise. Sadly, Dakota just sat on the sideline, wishing he was in there with his team… After some of our tough losses, I pulled the kids aside and showed them how to stop that from happening next time. I think we learned a lot today and matured some, too.

During one of the final matches, I saw a Southington kid wrestling well, and he certainly looked like he had a victory all wrapped up. But then, all of a sudden, late in the match, his opponent caught him in a cradle and pinned him. It shocked everyone, including the kid himself, who slapped the mat in frustration after losing. Then I heard a woman sitting near me, mutter in disgust, "Doesn't he remember the Douchebag Speech?" Wow! She must have been a Southington mother. And I guess Derek's speech really was impactful on their families over there… Maybe Derek should give that speech everywhere…

Well, it's dark out again as we board the bus, just like it was when we came here this morning. We're looking forward to our beds and another great week of wrestling ahead of us...

Brian Preece: When I was a head coach at Provo High School, I really took advantage of those that wanted to come in and work out with our wrestlers. BYU was a stone's throw from our high school.

Many young coaching interns and just guys that wanted to help out and work out would come over to see if they could work out with our boys. Many came for just a day or two, but some had a lasting impact. And I did the same thing they did when I broke into coaching. When my wrestling career was over at BYU, I just walked across the street and talked with the head wrestling coach, Gary Roylance. He was about my Dad's age and knew my Dad and knew of me. He was glad to have me on board, and since I was a coaching intern, I got some college credit.

One of my teammates from BYU, Jess Christen, actually became the head coach the next year as Gary would step down. I even got paid that year a stipend of $1000, which was pretty good money for a college kid in 1987. It was actually $100 better than the stipend I got for helping out at a high school 20 years later. I helped out for three years. After I graduated, I relocated to Salt Lake, where I got my first teaching job at West High School. West High was the most diverse high school in Utah, right in the heart of downtown Salt Lake City.

So through my experience as a coaching intern, I really knew how beneficial these young coaches could be for my athletes. Again, maybe some came for a practice or two, but some did have some lasting impact. Some were actual formal interns meaning they were expected to work the entire season, or perhaps when the semester ended in December depending on things, for college credit. But others were just former high school wrestlers that weren't on BYU's team. (It should be noted that BYU would drop its program in 2000. But as I said in our last book, wrestling is a popular sport among Mormons or members of the Church of Jesus Christ of Latter-day Saints. So the university was littered with hundreds of former high school wrestlers.)

I thought I would go the extra mile to give these interns, and those that might be interested in being high school coaches or that I might think could be good high school coaches, as full an experience as possible so they could learn the craft of coaching. It meant that I would let go of some things and let these young college kids instruct and teach techniques. But for some of the really serious ones, I tried to teach them the ins and outs of running a wrestling program like all the wonderful paperwork and fundraising, etc. that comes with the job.

I got to work with a lot of great people by opening up my room. I know some coaches are really reluctant to have people come into their room. And I see their point. And on occasion, I had a young kid (or two) that I had to not invite back. Sadly, they were there for their own egos versus helping the high school wrestlers or the program. But most were great.

I got to work with Jim Dandy Jr., a Native American from the Navajo Nation who later would become a head coach at Monument Valley (Utah). His father, like mine, was a high school teacher and coach, and Jim Jr. is still in the profession.

A couple of my student teachers were wrestlers, and not only did they do a day of Social Studies teaching for me, but they would also come down to the wrestling room. Phillip Morris and William (Bill) Turgeon both come to mind. They were great. Phillip is now an assistant principal at a northern Utah high school. Sadly Bill passed away last year after battling cancer. He became a college professor. Another one of my more reliable interns, Scotty Norton, sadly suffered the same fate. He became a head wrestling coach in Salt Lake valley, briefly coaching the first state champion in the history of that high school (Copper Hills). The boy he coached to a state title was actually the son of one of my college teammates. He then relocated back to his home state Michigan and tragically died way too young. I have to say it, cancer sucks!

Two of my best college interns/volunteers (to be later paid much like I was) were twin brothers, Chad, and Travis Blevins. Travis was actually dating the sister of one of my wrestlers. And by the way, the romance took, and the two are still very happily married. He was a California state qualifier who I think won one or two matches. Now, in Utah, it isn't necessarily a big deal to be a state qualifier. But in California, where 38 wrestlers qualify in a weight class where there are close to 800 wrestling schools, it is an achievement. So I had a good feeling about this young man and his technique.

The very next day, he comes in with someone who looks just like him, his brother Chad. Both were great, though, Chad really dived in as he wanted to be a high school teacher and coach. Travis would take a slightly different life path and go into elementary education. Chad really became a fixture in the high school wrestling scene, and I highly recommended him for the head wrestling coach position at a county rival high school called Mountain View. He became the head coach for a few years. Then got into administration, serving as the school's athletic director. He also became involved with the state association and running our state wrestling tournament. And as life would have it, he's my boss of sorts now. I retired from teaching and coaching for a year, but this past summer, he asked me to take on the challenge of being the boys' golf coach at their school. Their program has struggled over the years and only had four returning players on the roster, one of which chose not to play this year. But it has been fun being reunited with Chad in a different role. Sometimes with Chad (and my other interns that are still coaching and contributing to the sport), I refer to him as "my young Padawan, now Jedi Master." It's our inside joke of sorts.

But I have to say, much like what Daniel has found, it's not as easy to just coach anymore, whether being an official head coach or just a volunteer assistant. You just can't volunteer anymore, and Utah has pretty much the same hoops to jump through as Daniel has found in Connecticut. But to get back into coaching, I had to watch videos and pass tests on subjects like bullying, sexual harassment, blood-borne pathogens, financial, and travel policies. Luckily, I had a coaching minor, or I would have had to take a coaching course that Daniel mentioned. I also had to re-up my First Aid/CPR training, and of course, have the background check and fingerprinting.

The aggravating thing is that besides this golf coach gig, I took an online teaching position in my former school district, where I worked for 25 years. So I'm an employee of two different but neighboring school districts. But it didn't matter; within the space of six weeks, I had to rewatch pretty much the same videos and retake the same type of tests. I am still in total disbelief that with our technology and so forth, why districts or the Utah State Office of Education can't find a way to share information. So within a several-week period, I did basically the same battery of tests and went through two background checks and fingerprinting sessions. We're making it real hard for a college kid to help out a program, or in Daniel's case, be a volunteer coach as a Dad.

As far as coaching, generally, for head coaches in wrestling, the amount of paperwork and policy is enormous. It's not easy, in our state, at least, to do an overnight trip. All hotel and van rentals have to be approved by "State Travel." Every purchase is scrutinized. And specific to wrestling coaches, wrestlers' weights have to be tracked after the joys of taking your athletes through hydration testing. It's no accident that fewer and fewer people want to teach and coach. Schools are now relying more and more on paraprofessionals. And paraprofessionals rarely last long as coaches

CHAPTER THREE

DON'T MISS THE BUS!

Dan Blanchard: Monday, Dakota and I drove to practice together because he has this week off from school. I finally got to practice on time because I didn't have to do the hour drive from work. On the way to practice, Dakota shared with me again how bad he wants to be fixed and back on the mat. I totally understood what he was talking about because I wished I was fixed too from all my injuries and back on the mat again wrestling at full speed. Times seemed so much simpler back then when all I worried about was staying in shape and just wrestling.

On the ride over, I shared with Dakota, injured or not, that he has to be engaged at practice. He has to walk around the mat coaching his teammates and contributing to the team's success somehow. He said that frustrates him because he keeps telling the new kids the same things repeatedly, like, "Get in a better stance," we both say in unison. Then we both sprout off with, "Get your head up! Don't reach! Short arms!" I share Dakota's moment of frustration and tell him how that's what I'm doing too. And that we have to tell someone something 150 times before they finally get it. So, I guess we'll just keep telling them.

Practice went pretty well. We had twelve out of our twenty kids there today at the beginning of our school vacation week. By today's standards, the numbers weren't too bad. And due to the very workable numbers of just twelve kids spread among three coaches and Dakota, our player-coach, we were able to give the wrestlers a lot of individual attention today. Our 126-pounder is starting to turn the corner in his maturity and development. He has been wrestling well lately. I spent some time today showing him some things that would add to what he's already doing, and he picked up on it pretty fast. He had a great practice today. He should do well next weekend at the RHAM Duals.

Overall, it was a good practice and fun, too. Since I got there on time today, I was able to participate in the team warmup. During the warmups, I even hit a cartwheel and round-off during the line drills with only some minor discomfort in my shoulders. I'm feeling good and even a little younger after these acrobatics. I am so glad to be back on the mat, even if I am partially broken from a lot of wear and tear over the years.

Dakota looked pretty engaged today, too, through sharing what he knows with the newer wrestlers. Due to it being vacation week, at the end of practice, Coach Torres had the wrestlers do some pretty fun running and yelling drills like they were some kind of crazy warriors. It was fun. This activity worked on their air and lung capacity. All in all, I'd say it was a pretty good practice for the wrestlers that were there.

Tuesday, Christmas Eve, we moved practice up to the morning hours in consideration of team parents and their family plans. Unfortunately, Head Coach Torres couldn't make that earlier time slot because of work. So, Coach Rogers and I ran practice for the mere six wrestlers that showed up, which didn't really surprise me. Coach Rogers and I looked at each other and talked about how we still remember having three to four deep in every weight class when we wrestled. And some college kids would come back over the holidays to wrestle, too. It was common to see 50 kids in our old wrestling rooms during those times over our Christmas breaks.

Well, as Coach Torres said on the bus last Saturday, "We'll go with what we have." The bright side is that each of these six kids will learn something today. However, practice seems a little weird without Dakota. He is across the street at physical therapy. He will come over for the second half of practice and help out with some coaching since he still cannot wrestle.

Practice went pretty well, and as I figured, each of our six kids did indeed learn something today. We didn't figure on, though, that each of our kids got banged up some today. However, they still somehow managed to make it to the end of practice and have some fun. Even though we don't like it, being banged up is just part of wrestling. I even re-pulled a hamstring that has been bugging me on and off.

About two-thirds of the way through practice, I looked up at the clock and was surprised that Dakota wasn't there yet. I wondered if he was having an extra-long physical therapy session because his knee has been acting up again. Come to think of it, so has mine... Practice continued, and at the end of conditioning, we needed another body for Monkey Rolls, so I jumped in. I didn't know how I would do, but what I did know was that the team needed me. So, I was going to do it, regardless. One of our female wrestling managers blew the whistle, and Monkey Rolls began. Surprisingly, I hung in there with our youthful wrestlers just fine, and we ended practice on a good note. However, I was still wondering what happened to Dakota…

While changing after practice, I checked my phone and found out that Dakota had been locked out of the school building. He had been just standing out there for a long time, waiting for someone to come get him. He texted both Coach Rogers and me to come let him in, but neither of us had our phone on us during practice. We both felt terrible knowing that Dakota was here but couldn't get in because the doors were locked, and no other person in our building noticed him out there. We didn't have to lock our doors for added security measures when I was a young wrestler. I guess this is another issue with modern times. Poor Dakota… Life isn't always easy, and it often doesn't look the way we envision how it should be.

Well, Christmas comes and goes, and so does a couple more days of practice with about a dozen kids at each one. Dakota, his teammates, and his coaches are still frustrated going into Saturday's team duals tournament that he still cannot wrestle. Maybe Dakota needs to do more physical therapy on his own. Or perhaps he just needs more time to heal. After all, his doctor did say it would be a four-month recovery, which leads him up to the end of January or maybe even the beginning of February.

Also, even though Dakota is not wrestling at this Saturday tournament, we check his weight, wondering where he's at since he hasn't been able to do any workouts, and it's the holidays. Dang… he's ten pounds over again… I look him in the eye and say, "Dude, you got to start bringing your weight down."

The team tournament at RHAM in Hebron was another great wrestling tournament. However, it was a different experience for both Dakota and me this year. For Dakota, he was more of a spectator than a wrestler. For me, last year, I was a parent, not a coach. And at one point during the tournament last year, me and Dakota's mom snuck out and got a great sandwich down the road at a lovely little sandwich shop. No sneaking out this year as a coach, though. I have a job to do! And I, Coach Torres, and Coach Rogers, have a pretty big job to do today since a lot of our team is missing. We have seven wrestlers today. And we're giving up seven forfeits going into each team meet. That means that if all seven of our wrestlers pinned their kids, then we would at best earn a tie. It's going to be a winless day, no matter what we do. But the battle must go on!

The team tournament went well. And it was run very well by my old friend and former East Hartford Wrestler Ryan Fitch with a little help in the background from another old buddy and former East Hartford wrestler Kevin Kanaitis. Our first match was even against my dear old buddy, and fellow tri-captain wrestling teammate from the old days, Todd Albert of East Hartford High.

Our match against my old high school went good and bad, just like the three matches that followed. Because of all the forfeits we gave up today, we technically lost all four wrestling meets. The good thing is that in head-up matches, we actually won a lot more matches today against every team we wrestled than we lost. I kept joking with Coach Torres and Coach Rogers that we were both 0-4 and 4-0 today. I thought our kids wrestled very well, and I'm proud of all of them. They're moving closer toward becoming good young men.

Dakota did a nice job today by being engaged and offering coaching advice to his teammates. I also got to hang out a bit with my old friend and teammate, Todd Albert, from East Hartford. Todd shared an old digital picture he had on his phone of our old 1988 senior year wrestling team where I, Todd Albert, and Scott Buffington were tri-captains of the team. Upon seeing the picture, Coach Torres commented that we all looked buffed and tough. I mentioned that we all looked so young, too.

The day was enjoyable, and so was the bus ride home. The coaches were trading stories and laughing, and so were the wrestlers and the wrestling managers. The bus ride is a great place to build team spirit and unity, which builds stronger relationships. When the bus finally arrived back at school, my wife was waiting to pick Dakota and me up. Lately, I've been having a lot of car trouble. And my wife Jenn has been stepping up and bringing Dakota and me back and forth to wrestling when needed. It really does take a village to raise a kid and perhaps help a father, too. And it also really does take a village to raise a wrestler and possibly help a coach, too… even if it is just providing a ride…

Brian Preece: Daniel's writing had my mind buzzing. I first thought about bus rides as a coach, competitor, and even as a young boy traveling with my father as he took his team out to Steamboat Springs, Colorado, for a big wrestling tournament. I was about ten years old at the time and so excited to go with my Dad on a wrestling adventure. My Mom was pretty excited, I'm sure, to have one less kid to take care of for a weekend. I also learned that my Dad could be a bit of a hard-ass coach.

Two of his star wrestlers were late for the bus. Vernal, Utah, is about a three-hour drive from Steamboat Springs if the winter weather and road conditions are favorable. You take U.S. Highway 40 that connects Denver, Colorado to I-80, about 30 miles from Salt Lake City. Vernal is about 180 miles from Salt Lake and about 330 miles from Denver, relatively close to the Utah/Colorado border. So Uintah High School, the high school located in Vernal, wrestled a lot of schools on what they called the Western Slope of the Rockies or western Colorado. Uintah would often wrestle against Moffat County High School in Craig, Colorado, where my Dad graduated high school. Craig is about 120 miles east of Vernal on Highway 40, and Steamboat is another 40 miles or so east of that. Though Steamboat Springs is much like Aspen or Vail, known for its superb skiing and being a tourist trap, at that time, it had an outstanding wrestling program. I don't think that is much the case anymore as the town has got a bit wealthier and even touristier. However, back then, the town still had a rural/cowboy flavor and tough kids that would mix it up on the mat.

My Dad was pretty disgusted that these wrestlers were late. This was before the era of cell phones, so communication with athletes was much harder. There were a few attempts to call the parents and maybe a few other people to find their whereabouts. But it became time to leave, and my Dad was angry. The chances of winning the tournament were significantly reduced. Our bus had driven to about a small town on the Utah/Colorado border called Dinosaur, Colorado (yeah, that's its real name. Dinosaur fossils and the Dinosaur National Monument can be found in this region of Utah and Colorado) when a pick-up truck began honking and flashing its lights. My Dad had the bus driver pull over, and the pick-up truck pulled just ahead of the bus on the highway's shoulder. It was the two wrestlers.

My Dad was fuming, and the wrestlers were very apologetic. As they turned back toward their truck, my Dad said, "What the hell are you doing!" The wrestlers wanted to follow the bus to the tournament." My Dad spat out, "The hell you will. If you want to wrestle and be part of this team, grab your stuff and get your ass on the bus!" (My Dad could be coarse at times). So the two wrestlers grabbed their bags, and their truck was left on the side of the highway. I figured their parents or something would come to retrieve the vehicle.

Unitah won the tournament, the two wrestlers claimed gold medals, and I had a fun time hanging out with the wrestlers. This is where I learned that at that time in his coaching career, my Dad made his wrestlers eat the same meal, Chicken Fried Steak with all the fixins. Though it probably wasn't considered healthy then and certainly not now, I learned to like Chicken Fried Steak with all of the fixins'. The roads were often icy in the winter, so the team often stayed over on Saturday nights and went back home Sunday morning. So back we went to Vernal early Sunday morning. It was fun, and I liked to bother the wrestlers on the bus, and they liked to pick on me a bit. My Dad didn't care too much; he thought they and I both deserved it.

When we approached Dinosaur, the two late wrestlers desperately tried to get my Dad's attention. "Coach, we need to stop for our truck…" There was no stopping. My Dad simply told them, "Get your truck on your own damn time." Perhaps in the mid-1970s, there were still concerns over liability and athletes traveling in their own cars. But I don't think my Dad was much concerned about that. There was a lesson to be taught, and it was, "don't be late for the bus!"

Of course, I have to give these two wrestlers (and their parents) some amount of credit. I imagine in these times, some parents would have been offended that my Dad was so hard on their children that he cussed at them, made them leave their property on the side of the road, etc. Today, there would be meetings with administrators or even calls for my Dad's job. But the 1970s was a different era. In fact, the parents would later apologize to my father on behalf of their children. And the two wrestlers were among my Dad's all-time favorite wrestlers. Their relationship remained fully whole and intact. They loved their coach, and their coach loved them. And both ended up being state champions on a state championship team.

I thought bus rides, especially my senior year, were interesting experiences. Most of our meets were short trips, maybe a half-hour at the farthest. Wrestling is quite different from many sports because after the match is over, there will be wrestlers that have won and wrestlers that have lost. It's a little bit different than say, a football or baseball team, where all the team will feel "the thrill of victory, or the agony of defeat." The loss might not be as painful for some that won their bouts, and on the flip side, the team victory might be hollow to some wrestler that maybe got pinned in 30 seconds. And there were a few times on our bus ride home my senior year that my teammate (who would take state) and I were the only ones that won our matches in that dual meet. Maybe there were a couple of others. But I remember two duals where we lost 60-12 or something close to that. And the JV matches didn't go much better. So it wasn't that I felt I could or should be loud and celebratory on the bus. But overall, the bus rides I took as an athlete and coach were fun. We swapped many stories about girls, school, teachers, music, wrestling, parents, and life in general on those rides. It is that time to build stronger friendships with your teammates.

I genuinely applaud Daniel's (and Dakota's) efforts to keep Dakota engaged as he deals with his injury. It's hard for a coach to find things to keep an injured athlete engaged that are truly meaningful to the injured athlete and the team. And then the athlete has to buy-in. I look back at my coaching career and realized that sometimes I did well with this and sometimes not so much. There is so much benefit from keeping athletes involved. I hope Dakota will use this time valuably to remain close to his teammates and still continue to learn wrestling.

CHAPTER FOUR

FIGHTING DISCOURAGEMENT

Dan Blanchard: It's still the holiday vacation, but wrestlers don't really get this time off. Some people travel during the holidays. But the only traveling wrestlers usually do is back and forth to a bunch of wrestling practices and a few tournaments. Sure some wrestlers are forced by their parents to go on vacation during the holiday week. But most wrestlers don't go anywhere except for wrestling. The wrestlers also spend a lot of time visiting their bathroom scales because they still need to make weight. They have to watch what they eat and run off whatever they do eat at their family holiday gatherings.

A wrestler's life is a life of discipline and sacrifice. A wrestler can't give in to their everyday natural human urges of eating a lot and laying around. With its prehistoric roots, our brain always wants to preserve itself, and the holy temple called the body, which surrounds it and protects it. Thus, human beings are set up to eat a lot and preserve energy by moving around as little as possible to conserve calories, store fat, and live through lean times.

This prehistoric human inclination mentioned above of life-saving fat packing isn't beneficial to a wrestler. And neither are the holidays with all of its food. Yet, wrestlers are humans and do have families, so they must partake in the holiday season's festivities while trying to balance it all out. If they don't balance it well, they will be found bent over the trash can the next day at practice. And still overweight even though they just unwillingly emptied the excessive contents of their stomachs. Oh yeah, and there is always that other thing too: getting back to the rest of practice and finishing what one started. Wrestlers don't get to sit out of the rest of the practice just because they threw up.

However, sometimes even a wrestler's discipline and mandatory scheduled practices can't one-up Old Man Winter during the holiday season. Monday came this week, and so did snow and ice. All practices were called off by the school's athletic director. This is going to make making weight more challenging for our wrestlers.

Tuesday night was New Year's Eve, and we had wrestling practice. Dakota is still sidelined, and one can easily see that he is getting frustrated. I showed up for the first time this season in my street clothes. My wife told me not to get sweaty and to come home immediately after practice with Dakota. We had New Year Eve plans with family and friends. Oh, by the way, she had to bump back our plans to a later time because we were scheduled to have practice from 4-6 p.m. The non-wrestlers of the family, meaning everyone except Dakota and me, looked at us like we were crazy going to a New Year's Eve wrestling practice.

During that New Year's Eve practice, I found myself hanging out at the school building's front door again. Since I was the new coach, I had to let the wrestlers into the building while the two other coaches started practice. This had to be done because all the doors to the building were locked again, of course.

I'll repeat here again what I said last week. I don't like this new era where we have to take all these extra precautions for student and school safety. We continuously have to lock everything up. Well, come to think of it, I suppose I already should know better and already have accepted all these extra precautions. After all, I'm one of the district trainers where I teach school. Along with teaching students, I also train students and teachers on what to do if we have an active shooter in our building... Well... regardless... this former combat-trained military man turned husband, father, teacher, and wrestling coach once again still doesn't like the changes and extra precautions we have to face today.

When I finally walked into the back gymnasium, I could see the red wrestling mats' three sections with their nine little circles rolled out. Wrestlers were already warming up. I ran into a wrestler's mom who has been helping out with the team. She complimented Dakota, calling him a real trooper to be here every day even though he hasn't been able to wrestle. I agreed and told her that it's killing all of us, though.

Wednesday, January 1st, 2020, finally arrives! HAPPY NEW YEAR, EVERYONE! Today we take down all the holiday decorations and then head back over to our beloved high school for another wrestling practice. That's right! We have wrestling practice from 2-4 p.m. today. Time for the wrestlers, and me, too, to sweat off all that food from last night.

I'm looking forward to a little workout. Thanks to this wrestling season, I have relearned how to do a light jog. Due to an old injury and then a total hip replacement of my left hip, I have been physically unable to jog for the last decade. But now I can manage a short jog, and that feels pretty good. However, recently, I pulled a hamstring slowly running a few hills on my driveway before a wrestling practice last week. I mention to Dakota in passing that I sure hope my pulled hamstring doesn't hurt too much today in practice, and he says, "How do you think I feel?"

I reply, "Yeah... you're right. Sorry." I feel pretty stupid right about now for complaining to my son about a sore hammy.

On the car ride over to our first wrestling practice of the new year and new decade of the '20s, Dakota tells me that he will be really mad if he gets injured again next year. I say to him that he can't think about that. He has to think positive thoughts instead. Besides, wrestling isn't really about winning trophies. It's about building character and becoming a good young man.

He says, "Dad, how am I supposed to build character if I can't even wrestle?"

I respond, "You can build character through an injury, too. After all, don't they say that it's not what happens to you, but rather how you respond to it that really matters?" At this moment, I think about the wrestler's mom, who called Dakota a real trooper for being there every day even though he couldn't wrestle. A car suddenly cuts in front of me. My mind shifts gears, and I forget to share this with Dakota before we get to practice. I can't tell him right now either, because he's sleeping as I'm writing this in the wee hours of the morning. Well, I'm pretty sure he'll get the lesson when he reads my blog.

Now back to New Year's Day. Dakota surprises me on this New Year's Day practice by weighing in at only 140 lbs. He's lost a few pounds. He's now only six pounds over for his weight class that is now 134 lbs. I'm thinking cool, he still might be able to make weight by the end of the month even though he hasn't been able to work out. And if his doctor releases him at the end of the month, he might actually get a chance to wrestle a couple of matches and go to the State Tournament.

But Coach Torres drops a bomb on us. He says that if Dakota wants to wrestle in the States in mid-February, he needs to officially weigh in eight times at matches before the State Tournament. This means that he will have to be on weight and ready to go by next Saturday if he wants any chance of wrestling in the States this season. I'm caught off guard by this because I thought it was just one match before the States. My mind also goes back to last season when Dakota was out for six weeks with his knee the size of a softball leading up to States. It didn't look like he'd be able to wrestle at the end-of-the-season tournament either. Life is never easy…

Dang… what to do once again…? Hmm… not sure… However, just like last year, let's give it our best shot and see what happens. Somehow last year, at the eleventh hour, he did manage to wrestle in the States when his doctor cleared him and his knee at the last possible moment. Maybe, somehow, Dakota will pull it off again this year.

Now we have to get him moving again. Coach Torres gives Coach Rogers and me the okay to commodore an exercise bike from the schools' weight room. Rogers and I set the bike up right next to the wrestling mat and order Dakota to get on and start pedaling. Hopefully, this won't stress his knee too much. Hopefully, it will develop his leg muscle back up that has atrophied. Hopefully, it will build his wind.

And hopefully, it will bring his weight down some too. Let's do our best and hope for the best.

Dakota's bike ride went well. It tired him out, and now we're back home, icing his knee again. He's frustrated and asking me if I think he'll have any chance of wrestling this season, and if it's even possible for him to make weight if he is cleared. I encourage him through what I learned many years ago by reading General Colin Powell's book on his time in the Vietnam War. I let Dakota know that Powell always said to his men, "Things will look better in the morning." I tell Dakota not to make any decisions when he's tired and feeling beat up. Get a good night's sleep. Tomorrow morning he'll feel better, and then we'll talk about it.

The next morning is Thursday, and we have a wrestling match against Rocky Hill High School. This week, it is on a Thursday instead of the usual Wednesday because of the holiday. Jenn, Dakota's mom, can finally watch a wrestling meet, even though Dakota won't be wrestling. Jenn has been with our two youngest daughters every Wednesday and Saturday so far for soccer. So, it will be nice today for Dakota to look up in the stands and see his mom.

Instead of riding on the bus with the team, I ride down to Rocky Hill with my wife, Jenn. When we get there, I see my old friend Paul Myers, the head wrestling coach of Rocky Hill. I also see one of my old buddies from Bristol refereeing the match. Next, I see our team out on the mat warming up and Dakota sitting all by himself on the team bench. I don't think Dakota likes sitting on that bench too much. He's looking a little bit like a loner... and I'm not loving it too much either...

Tonight, some of our kids wrestle well, and some of them don't. Once again, our 126-pounder looks good, and so does our 138-pounder senior captain. Dakota knows the 132-pounder he would have wrestled from off-season wrestling. It would have been a good match. Using some strategy, we bump our 160-pounder to 170, and he pins his kid. Next, our 182-pound brawler goes out there. And once again does what he so often does by pinning his kid too. These were the bright spots, along with a few newer kids battling hard, but unfortunately coming up short.

The not-so-good spots, which Coach Torres made sure the whole team was well-aware of, were the losses we took that mostly came from kids that have been missing practices. Don't these kids know the old Woody Allen saying that showing up is fifty percent of the battle? One has to be consistent. One has to show up every day. And one has to work hard every day. And one has to always go the extra mile if one wants to be good in wrestling, well in life, and become a good man…

At the end of the meet, Coach Torres let the kids know that he wasn't happy and that tomorrow's practice would be a hard one. Then we head out onto the mat to show good sportsmanship by shaking hands with the other team.

After shaking hands with Rocky Hill, I briefly talked with my old comrade from Rocky Hill, Coach Myers, to catch up some. He mentions that he's been reading my blog and enjoying it. Very cool… Another great wrestler and a great coach who is getting something positive out of my wrestling blog… I'm pumped! I guess I'll keep pounding away on my computer keyboard…

Friday's practice was good and hard, just like Coach Torres said it would be. And on Saturday, we found ourselves over at Windham High School for the Windham Duals Wrestling Tournament. Unfortunately, we're going into this tournament as a huge underdog with all of our young newer kids, and the fact that we don't even have a full team. We are forfeiting five weight classes. In every one of those weight classes, we give the other team six-points instead of earning a possible six points for ourselves. If one knows the complicated math of wrestling, that's basically a 30-60 point shift in favor of the other team. Last week Saturday, we out-wrestled every team we faced but didn't win a single meet. We may not win a single meet today either… Hopefully, we'll at least out-wrestle the other teams though…

Unfortunately, we didn't out-wrestle the first team we went against. We lost again. Coach Torres yelled at the team, letting them know that if a few of them didn't get pinned, we might have had a chance to win this one because the other team had to give up a couple of forfeits themselves. The wrestlers that did get pinned were newer guys that truly don't belong in a varsity lineup. They should be on the freshmen team or junior varsity team, but unfortunately, we don't have that luxury. We asked a lot from these green wrestlers, and some may think that's not fair to them. And I sort of agree… But guess what? Life isn't going to be fair to them either. So, they might as well learn that fact now… Hey, I wrestled varsity as a freshman who had never wrestled previously either. And whenever I lost, my coach gave me hell for not manning-up out there…

The next three matches we wrestled, we did out-wrestle the other teams. And we actually won two of them! Our veterans performed well like they usually do. And our newbies sucked it up and came up with some big wins. These unexpected wins caused our wrestlers and parents to jump up and down and shout at the top of their lungs in jubilation. It was awesome! What a day!

And to add to this great day, a parent from another team introduced himself to me and told me that he thinks I'm really good with the kids. Pretty cool, huh? My wife also told me that the team moms are giggling and getting a kick out of the fact that whenever one of our kids loses, I don't yell at them, but instead enthusiastically pull them aside and show them how to better defend themselves for the next time. My wife just looks at the moms, and says, "He's always been like that."

I also had a pleasant surprise today when I was walking by a wrestling mat, and someone called out my name. I couldn't believe my eyes. It was my old buddy Tom Barry. Many times over the years, I've wondered what happened to him. Tom, who I wrestled my sophomore year. He was one of the top wrestlers in the state and the senior captain for Maloney High School in Meriden. Tom was an awesome wrestler. He even looked like an awesome wrestler, too, with that thick neck of his. We had a great battle that I believe ended up with him pinning me in the third period off of a fireman's carry. A few years later, we were hanging out on the coaching and refereeing circuit. He was one of the state's best referees.

We hung out a lot, and we're good friends, but life eventually took us in different directions. I got away from wrestling with my family and work responsibilities. And Tom stepped away from wrestling as well. He told me he's now a big baseball umpire. Kind of surprising, but not really when I think about it. I asked him what he was doing at this wrestling tournament, and he responded with how it's his therapy... "I hear you, buddy," I answered. We both sat quietly together for a few moments enjoying each other's company once again after all these years... Then duty called, one of my wrestlers was up, and I was off running...

Brian Preece: My Dad had a saying similar to the one Daniel quoted from General/Secretary Colin Powell. His saying when times were tough and things were discouraging is that "the sun will come up tomorrow." But my Dad had some times as a coach, especially when he was at Skyline High School, where times were tough and discouraging. Perhaps the most discouraged I saw my father, as a coach, was my senior year.

It was Thursday night and we had just lost a dual meet against the top team in our region (league) which was Granger High School. It was a real bad night as we lost 49-2. My teammate Jon Clark, who would later take State that year, won his match (barely) but my Dad lost a team point during the meet so that is why we only scored two points. The rest of us, including me, lost. I lost to my rival (and now friend) Pat Bradshaw, 3-2.

I would wrestle Pat five times my senior year. This was our third meeting. In our first meeting, he pinned me in the second round of the Layton Invitational. Then we met a week later in the championship finals of the Granite District Invitational and I beat Pat pretty good by seven or eight points. At that time I thought the first meeting was a fluke and I had things under control. Now this match with Pat, unlike our other four matches, was very low scoring. Most of our matches were high-scoring affairs as sometimes we would nearly put up 30 points combined. But this one was low scoring. I got a takedown, he got an escape and a takedown and I got rode out and lost.

My Dad was really frustrated. The bus ride home was long, quiet, and cold. And then our car ride home seemed even longer and definitely was quieter and colder. We pulled into the driveway and I could tell Dad was really pondering something.

We were heading out to wrestle Uintah High School, his former school, in a dual meet the next day. We were basically a struggling 4A school and Uintah was ranked at that time as the number one team in 3A. It was likely we were going to get crushed in this dual meet. My Dad had an ego, and he didn't want to get humiliated by his former school, which was now coached by one of his former assistant coaches. On top of that, our best wrestler had a football recruiting trip and wouldn't be going out with us.

So he asked me a sincere question, and to this day, I view this as one of my best moments as a competitor and human being. He asked whether we should cancel the trip. He just didn't think it was worth it to go out with a young and inexperienced team without one of its top wrestlers to battle against a top team. But I told him bluntly that "I wanted to go."

I looked forward to this scheduled trip to my former hometown with both excitement and trepidation. In regards to the latter, I felt huge immense pressure to do well, not just for myself but for my Dad. I had no delusions our team would win or do well. I knew I would be wrestling against one of my former youth teammates, who was always bigger than me growing up by several weight classes. So I was a bit nervous about that because when we were 11 years-old, it would have been easy for him to pound me into the ground, and I had to overcome that mindset a bit. So I didn't want to lose or do poorly.

The good part is that a good share of Uintah's team would be friends I grew up with and I just wanted to see some of these people. I knew a lot of other friends growing up would be there in the stands watching. I just thought it would be cool to wrestle in front of a packed house versus the empty gyms that were typical in our home meets and most of the time when we wrestled on the road. And back to the previous chapter I bit, I looked forward to spending time with my teammates on a bus, missing school, and showing off a bit where I grew up. So again, there was a lot of nervousness and excitement all rolled into one.

The meet itself went better than it did against Granger. No, we didn't win, in fact, we lost 50-10. We got a pin by our heavyweight and we actually had two ties. (Back then you could have ties in dual meets as there was no overtime). And guess what, I was one of those ties.

I wrestled my friend Kary McNiel and I got a takedown and put him right on his back with my patented outside (or Kelly) fireman's carry. So right off the bat, I went up 5-0. The rest of the match wasn't so great. I think Kary got an escape and a takedown in the second round to cut my lead to 5-3. I was suffering a bit from some self-doubt, having wrestled a tough opponent from the night before and lost and on top of that had a three-hour bus ride to my former home town, along with all the nerves of doing well for my father. I was then dinged for stalling for two points in the final round. The official for this meet was the coach that took over Uintah after my Dad left and now they weren't getting along too well. My Dad was a bit livid. At any rate, after six minutes of wrestling, the match ended up a draw. And I think I was more okay with it than Dad was at the time. In my heart, I knew Kary outwrestled me, but I also knew in my heart that I outscored him and at least one of those stalling calls a bit fishy as I was fighting off a pinning combination. But oh well. Kary wrestled great after being down 5-0 and I didn't lose at the time to the top-ranked wrestler in 3A. As it would turn out, Kary would finish third in the 3A state meet and I would finish fourth in 4A. And I think when we won the last match of the night that took a little sting out of things for our team and especially my Dad. I am glad, as a coach, to have had some good big men wrestlers.

And it was nice to see my old friends but for my Dad, he found out that the sun did come up from the night before even though victory was far from obtained. My Dad was able to show his team at Skyline the championship banners of teams he coached. Many parents of his former wrestlers came back to see their old coach. And though we headed back to Salt Lake a defeated team, our spirit wasn't defeated. Instead of not having a weekend of competing, we got a dual meet in my former hometown. I left in a good mood and my confidence a bit restored as I headed into the final stretches of what I thought would be my last matches as a competitor.

What was even nicer was one of the Uintah parents mailed out the newspaper (the Vernal Express) several days after the meet. It was typical of the small-town newspapers of rural America, the hub of the town was the high school. Several pages were dedicated to this dual meet and several photos of my father coaching and me competing, and a few of my friends wrestling from both teams. I grew up in the era of videotape and I don't have a lot of still photos of me wrestling. So I have always appreciated the efforts of sending those out to my Dad, and they are now in a scrapbook. Most importantly, I am proud of the fact, then and now, that I told my father we should go and do this meet. Though we didn't win as a team and my match ended up in a tie, returning to my hometown to compete still remains one of my favorite memories as a competitive wrestler. A few years later when my Dad had more competitive teams, he returned with my younger brother Scott to dual Uintah again and compete in the tournament he started at the school, the prestigious Uintah Tournament of Champions. He didn't win the dual meet or the tournament either, but all was good.

CHAPTER FIVE
THE COMPLEXITIES OF BEING A HIGH
SCHOOL WRESTLER AND COACH

Dan Blanchard: Week six is here, and the struggle for Dakota's knee to heal in time continues. We're hearing many different things from a lot of different people about what to expect for his recovery time and whether or not he'll be able to wrestle in the State Tournament at the end of the season. We're also going back and forth on what this all means for Dakota's off-season wrestling as well. I'm also kind of bumming it because in my sophomore year at 132-pounds, I had the whole season to wrestle with our 138-pound senior captain, and it made me a lot better. I was psyched that Dakota would also have this same opportunity as a sophomore. But unfortunately, surgery on his knee has destroyed that opportunity of growth for him. Life isn't fair.

I don't remember wrestling being this complicated when I was a high school wrestler. All I did was just wrestle. That's it. Just wrestle. We didn't have these mental acrobatics going on with, "Well, what if this happens?" or, "What if that happens?" It feels like it's just too much drama. I wonder if I'm feeling like this because I'm a wrestler parent now instead of the wrestler.

In a way, I hope it's because I'm a parent now. I hope Dakota is not going through all this drama too. Sadly, I find myself in conversations almost daily involving this topic of "what ifs" with my wife, who doesn't always see things as I do. And I know that some of these conversations are taking place either in front of Dakota. Or at least within ear-shot of him. I hope we're not stressing him out. Wrestling is hard enough, and being an injured wrestler certainly is hard enough without all the adults in one's life adding stress to it.

Well, like a trooper, even among all the craziness, I walk into practice on Monday and find Dakota riding the bike again on the side of the mat. He's trying to fight his way back up and hopefully bring his weight back down. The practice goes well. And we have our school's former first and only Open State Champion's father watching. He's there to pick up his daughter, one of the wrestling team's managers.

This phenomenon above is quite common in wrestling. Often a younger sister comes out to help manage the wrestling team. And then continues to stick around after her older brother graduates. I know it happened with my three younger sisters all those years ago. There is a solid bond in the wrestling world that makes people want to stick around.

The father of our team's first Open State Champion was a nice addition to practice on Monday. He kept yelling out to the kids encouraging them to work harder. It brought a nice vibe to the air. And I think everyone did work harder that day. As a matter of fact, I think we should have that father here more often. And he sure looked like he was having fun, too. He was great for team morale!

During the practice, one could see that Dakota was getting restless, though. He just didn't seem himself. I wasn't liking it much. I wish I could help him out of the tough spot he's in. But he has to carry most of the weight himself on this one. It's all part of wrestling, helping him become a better man by handling tough times and disappointments that are sure to continue well after his wrestling days are over.

During practice, Dakota came out onto the mat to show a younger wrestler a move. But then the two of them goofed off some, and Coach Rogers had to yell at him to get off the mat, be careful with his knee, and get back on the bike.

I don't think Dakota liked being yelled at… But, sometimes, that's what needs to be done… The strongest steel has to endure the hottest fires, right?

When I walked into the wrestling room on Tuesday, I saw Dakota alongside the mat on the bike, pedaling away again. I could see on his face that something was very wrong. I asked him about his weight, and it was still up there. So I wondered if he was worried that he wasn't dropping the weight fast enough.

No…, it seemed more than just a weight loss problem to me. But he wouldn't tell me what had him in such a funk. Later on, I found out that what was causing Dakota distress was one of the oldest problems of mankind. This problem has been around forever. And it happens to all of us men more often than we would like. Dakota was having some relationship challenges with his girlfriend… Geez… More drama… And once again, my heart breaks for him, but once again, there's nothing I can do about it…Dang.

It's crazy how much relationship problems can make it tougher to wrestle. I remember a time back in high school when I was having girlfriend problems. And how much it frustrated me one particular night when my opponent refused to stay pinned. It felt like the whole world was against me, life wasn't fair, and a lot of my strength had been stolen from me. I still won that match against the other team's captain. Heck, I think I might have even pinned him, but it sure felt like it was way harder to do it that night than it should have been.

Later in the week, Coach Scot Roger's wife, Val Rogers, will tell me that way back in their youth, Scot actually broke up with her once during wrestling season because he said the whole dating thing was a distraction. Scot wanted to focus solely on wrestling so he could do his best, and dating was taking some of his energy and attention away from wrestling, he thought. Thankfully, back in those days, most athletes, including Coach Rogers, didn't wrestle year-round. So the dating of Valerie would eventually be okay again. And that's a good thing because it led to their son, who is the 138-pound senior captain of our team this year. And he's an outstanding wrestler.

Okay, back to Dakota. On the car ride home, Dakota still wouldn't talk about it, but he did open up enough to talk about his physical therapy session of that day. His doctor and the physical therapist think his knee is making good progress. So, now they want to speed up the recovery of his right thigh muscle that had atrophied. His right quadricep is still noticeably smaller than his left. So, his medical team wants to try the tourniquet strategy on him.

I'm not familiar with the tourniquet strategy outside of what it meant to me in combat training during my time in the army as a frontline infantryman. So Dakota had to explain it to me. He shared how the tourniquet strategy slows down the blood flow. And this forces the thigh to work harder during exercise, which then causes the quadricep muscles to pop back out to regain some of its former size and shape. Regaining full strength would eventually follow later through a lot more resistance training.

This strategy sounded interesting. I'm looking forward to seeing the results. Although, I guess I'll have to get back to you later to let you know how well it works…

Wednesday night's match was much anticipated by everyone, including myself. We were going to my old battlegrounds, where I had terrorized the rest of the state during my wrestling days. We were wrestling at my alma mater East Hartford High School. We had already bumped up against my old team in an earlier tournament this season. We lost to them in points but outwrestled them in head-up matches. Tonight, we were hoping to do even better than just out wrestling them. However, we know that they will be making adjustments and be gunning for us this time around.

When I got to East Hartford High School, I saw that my son's team was already there and getting ready to warm up for the match. I also saw my old buddy, Todd Albert, the head wrestling coach of East Hartford. Todd was my former teammate who had also been a captain with me of our 1988 team. Later on that night, I will learn from Todd's wife, Kim, that Todd had just won his 100th match as a head wrestling coach. Todd is so modest. I wish he had told me right then and there so I could have congratulated him right there on the spot.

I also ran into a few other old East Hartford friends I went to high school with, Kelly Boyd and Jason Bedard. Kelly and I had a great talk before the match, where I learned her boy would be wrestling our 138-pound senior captain, the son of Coach Rogers and his wife, Valerie. As I mentioned earlier, he's pretty good, so I gave my old friend Kelly a heads-up that her boy would have a tough match. After the meet was over, I ran into Jason Bedard, whose boy wrestled our jayvee 120-pounder. His boy was only 111-pounds and brand new, so it was a really tough match for him too as he also lost to one of our boys. However, I'm sure it was a good learning experience for both Kelly and Jason's sons that night.

It was great seeing my old buddies Todd, his assistant coach Nick. Nick is another East Hartford former wrestling, which I've come to know better over the last several years. And it's always great to see old friends like Kelly and Jason again.

However, what was not so great that night was that we got outwrestled on the same East Hartford mats that I used to own as a wrestler in my youth. East Hartford had a much larger team than we had and thus had some strategic options available. Many of our guys who won last time went up against different East Hartford kids this time and lost. We made a lot of rookie mistakes, and East Hartford capitalized on many of them. Coach Rogers was upset that we were looking into half-nelsons all night long. Coach Torres was mad that some of our kids were being pushed around out there. And I was frustrated that nothing seemed to go our way tonight.

Well, to be honest with you, there were actually at least a few things that did go our way tonight. First, our female wrestler who we bumped up to the 170-pound class wrestled a boy who was a lot bigger than her. No one thought she had a chance. But she went out there and pinned him. One of our struggling jayvee kids pinned his kid too. These were great moments of the night that at least momentarily pumped us all up.

Oh, yeah... and there was also one more thing. Every now and then I overheard voices of people saying, "Hey, Coach Blanchard had once wrestled at this school." That was kind of cool. Our 160-pounder approached me and said out loud that he's pretty sure that this is the school that I used to wrestle at. That was even cooler, especially when I answered that it was. And it was also the school that I won two wrestling state championships and one football state championship. I figured he would like that since he was also both a football player and a wrestler.

On the way out the door, another former East Hartford wrestler, Tyler LeBlanc, who refereed tonight's match, told me he did some homework. He had asked some other referees about how the rules apply to Dakota's situation of being injured regarding the States. He told me that the rule says Dakota has to participate in eight matches to go to the States. And that participation means more than just weighing in and then forfeiting his matches until he's ready to wrestle again. He has to actually wrestle in eight meets... Dang... another one of our plans blown out of the water again. Things just got a little bleaker for Dakota.

Things keep getting crazier. It's Thursday, and I've been waiting for word from my wife, Jenn, on what the doctor said about Dakota today. On the drive home, my phone finally rings, and it's Jenn with bad news. She tells me the doctor said it will be another month before he releases Dakota to wrestle.

I sigh and say, "Well, I guess that's it. Dakota's season is over." Another month will put us way too close to the States for Dakota to still get in his eight official matches.

However, there is still something bugging me. My old comrade and teammate, John Knapp from KT KIDZ in Rocky Hill, with whom I wrestled in the Junior Olympics, still thinks Dakota can just show up at the States and wrestle. Also, an email I received from Steve Merlino, the President of the CIAC said that it was a layered answer. However, after sifting through his email, it sort of looks like Dakota might still be able just to show up and wrestle in the States. As long as he makes weight for the weight class he was certified for at the beginning of the season, he may still be able to wrestle.

Jenn says that Dakota is upset and wouldn't even talk to her on the ride home from the doctors' office. I can't blame him for being frustrated, but he should have at least manned-up enough to talk to his mom on the way home. However, I know that's easier said than done. Heck, I'm getting stressed out by this season too, so I can only imagine what it must be doing to the teenage boy going through it.

I finally arrive at practice to see how Dakota is doing, and I once again see him on the bike. "Good," I think. He hasn't thrown in the towel yet. He's still trying to rehabilitate his knee, get in shape, make weight, and be part of this team.

After I see Dakota, I next go see Coach Torres and Coach Rogers. Both are wondering, "What the heck just happened?" And I can't blame them either for this disbelief and frustration. They've got a pretty good wrestler who could have helped the team win some matches this year just sitting on the bench.

"What are we going to do, coaches?" I ask them.

"He's going to make weight. We're going to officially weigh him in starting this Saturday. And we're bringing him to the State Tournament with our fingers crossed," quipped Coach Rogers with a little bit of a fire in his eyes.

I was happy to see that we would do everything that we could and then let the chips fall where they will. However, I know Dakota will have trouble making the 134-pound weight class just two days from now. I wish he had followed my advice and brought his weight down one pound a week starting a month ago. I know that's a hard thing to do during the holiday season, especially when you're injured and can't wrestle. But sometimes you just have to figure out how to do something now, so later it becomes easier. Pay now so you can play later. Or you play now, but you'll then have to pay later.

I had to leave practice early today because I had to go record my weekly Mindalia TV show. I interview people from all over the world on some of the great things they're doing to make the world a better place. So, I didn't get to see Dakota again until later that night back at home. My wife, Jenn, told me that Dakota was still in a bad mood. I approached him and asked him what his weight was after practice.

He said, "145-pounds." My heart sank again. It's over. There's no way he'll make the 134-pound weight class in just 36 hours from now. This season is driving me crazy.

Then all of a sudden, I notice the corners of Dakota's mouth drawing up a bit. And Jenn's too, but not as dramatically as Dakota's "Hey, what's going on here?" my facial expression asks. Dakota smiles and says that he's actually on weight. He weighed 133.8 pounds after practice today. Jenn and Dakota were messing with me, and they almost got me on that one. Well, maybe they did get me a little bit...

After releasing a colossal smile myself, I blurt out, "How is that even possible?" Dakota smiles and says that he thinks he lost six or seven pounds riding the exercise bike today. I can't believe it. "How the heck did he do that?" is all I can think. After I gather myself, I blurt out, "You're going to make weight on Saturday!"

Maybe not... I arrive at practice on Friday and approach Dakota on his exercise bike at the side of the mat once again to ask him what his weight is, and he answers that it's 138 point something.

Dang... I knew Dakota making weight yesterday was too good to be true. I feared that he'd be back up today. And now my fears have come true...

This week's Saturday tournament was really cool. We went to the 9th Annual Casey Yates Invitational Tournament with 14 other teams. It was held at my wife, Jenn's alma mater, Lyman Memorial, where she was the first graduating class from that building when it was new.

Casey Yates was a former Lyman wrestler. He had become very good at wrestling after attending one of Shirzad Ahmadi's summer camps, his mom told me. Casey was also an accomplished scholar in high school and college, graduating from the University of Hartford summa cum laude. He had a great sense of humor and was also a singer and songwriter who released several original CDs. He was a postbaccalaureate pre-med student at the University of Texas at Dallas when an accident took him from all of us way too soon.

I had a wonderful conversation with Casey's mom, Marie Quinn, and Becky, who was also working behind the memorial table. They were such a delight to talk to. Marie and Becky really got it when I talked about some of the trials and tribulations of being a parent to a wrestler. They are both a testament to people finding a community through wrestling and then sticking around to continue to do good in this world. My hat goes off to Marie, Becky, and the hundreds of others who make this annual tournament possible and who are out there doing good on a daily basis. We miss you, Casey. Keep shining your goodness down on all of us, my fellow warrior.

We had a pretty good day at the tournament. Dakota actually made weight somehow. Our 138-pound senior captain took first. Our 182-pounder dramatically won the first-place trophy through a really cool move that pinned his opponent in the finals' first period. Our 160-pounder took third. And our 113-pounder, first-year wrestling shocked and rocked that gymnasium with his gutsy performance that landed him in the medal rounds of fighting for 3rd and 4th place. We also had several other of our young wrestlers show some guts out there and win a few matches.

I even got to share this pretty cool day with my wife and two youngest daughters as they came and hung out with us wrestlers before and after their soccer games.

It was also a great day because CIAC President Stephen Merlino showed up. And I was able to speak to him one-on-one to clarify his email about Dakota's situation. He basically said that as long as Dakota is healthy, gets ten practices in, and makes his certified weight class, he can still wrestle in the States. How freaking cool is that? There is still hope!

It was a very long day, but a great day for our team. We got back on our team bus for the second time that day in the dark. We were all tired but satisfied with the day. Coach Rogers commented on the bus ride home that Dakota must be biting at the bit to wrestle again after watching a day of wrestling like this one. And he was. And I know this is true because he told me so on the car ride home from our high school without me even asking him about it. Once again, there is still hope…

Even after all the craziness, it was a good week of wrestling. I'd like to leave you all now with a poem from an unknown author that Casey Yates' mom Marie Quinn gave to me.

The Wrestling Parent

Parents in wrestling are courageous – it's true:
They feel all the pain that their boys must go through.
At home, when he diets, they wish it could stop,
Yet know he must do it to stay on top.

Excuses for losing they will never endure,
"Don't blame the ref, son, because of the score.
The coach, he will show you the best way to move,
Keep working in practice if you want to improve."

At dual meets you'll see them whispering a prayer,
As their boys must compete with no one else there.

Whatever the outcome- Mom cheers with deep pride,
While Dad- you will notice- stands right by his side.

They'll drive to a tournament; many miles away,
To witness a son who's prepared for this day.
Their boy, he has trained, with all of his might,
Having hopes of becoming a champion tonight.

But should he fall short, at his corner you'll find,
A Mother and Father- supportive and kind.
They teach that through wrestling he'll learn about life,
Yes, living is filled with both triumph and strife.

Now if you are searching for people who care,
Just look by a mat, they'll always be there.
Such love for the sport is truly inherent,
That's why we salute, The Wrestling Parent!

Brian Preece: Girl, girls, girls! They tended to avoid me like the plague growing up. I was no ladies' man. I didn't marry my high school sweetheart. I didn't even have a high school sweetheart. But I know girls and dating can be a huge distraction for a high school wrestler and weigh on the emotions of the teenage mind. Heck, it can even weigh on the emotions of the adult mind as it did to me. I was so bad at dating and romance in high school, there wasn't much issue there. No girl to get my insides in a twist, not too much. There was this girl I was sweet on in high school. We went to Homecoming our senior year but no romance kindled. We have stayed in touch over the years, she's a wonderful person. She actually married somebody in our friend group, a great guy and I think they have adopted three or four kids. Really amazing people.

I was more in a twist about women in my coaching years. The opposite also evaded me (ha-ha) in college, but I think I started to get better at the dating scene a bit over time. Maybe. I remember when I moved from West High School, where I was an assistant wrestling coach, to take my first head coaching job at Provo High School, I scheduled a meet with West High School and I admit it was fun to see many of these West High wrestlers again. But some quickly noticed I was different-physically.

"Coach, you've lost a lot of weight," said one of my wrestlers I used to coach. And I did. When I was at West HS I bounced between 220 and 230 pounds. But I remember getting on the scale for fun and was weighing 189 pounds. But it wasn't a healthy weight loss. My new job as a head coach was stressing me out, my teaching demands were stressing me out, my hour-long commute home was stressing me out, and mostly my dating life was stressing me out. And who knows if I was "dating" anyone in the literal definition of dating. I was put in the "friend zone" but always wanted more, and I was the gentleman and paid for all the dinners. But the desire of wanting this relationship to be something more was causing me to not eat, not sleep and just stress.

I have no idea how I survived my first year at Provo High School. I had some good friends like my assistant coach Darren Hirsche. And in Salt Lake my good friend Erik Holdaway, who I met in college. They were my best friends and always there to be a listening ear. But I was mostly just younger and healthier. Just adrenaline I guess and maybe I wasn't the best classroom teacher either that year. I can admit that. Something had to give I guess. I remember every night driving back between 6:00 and 7:00 p.m., if not later, to Salt Lake from Provo, about a 40-mile drive that could take up to an hour or depending on traffic and road conditions.

I look back now thinking how crazy this was. So I did my best to have a social life, I even had season tickets to the Utah Jazz. Yes, tickets plural, you know, for dating. Though most often I would take my friend Erik to the games. I remember trying to go to bed between midnight and 1:00 a.m. and my alarm would go off at 5:50 a.m... I was usually out the door between 6:20 and 6:30 a.m., but I wasn't much of a morning person. Let's just say I wasn't one of those teachers in my classroom 30 minutes before the first bell rang. But I figure maybe some grace could be given because I was coaching three sports, often chaperoned dances and other events, and was most often at the school 11 hours at the minimum, maybe close to 14 to 15 hours on other days. Again, I guess you have a lot more energy at 29 years old than 55.

I remember this relationship finally ending for good and I got into another relationship my second year at Provo High School which carried a bit into my third year. But I was put into the "friend zone." One thing I would always advise anyone and Dakota in this case-don't go into the "friend zone" because it's just going to be painful in the end 99 out of 100 times. It is going to be prolonged anxiety and agony. Especially if you're in your 20's and 30's, either the relationship is going forward towards something, or it isn't. Maybe teens can wait it out but even then expect an emotionally exhausting journey. Best to make a clean break. But these young ladies loved me as a friend, while I would always hope for more (and spend a lot of money on them hoping for more). And I don't think dating and/or courtship should be a lot of "work" or be emotionally draining. To me, that's a good sign that things are amiss and a love connection doesn't exist.

Then in my third year of teaching, in late October just before wrestling season was going to officially start, I met my wife Heidi. She was student-teaching in the special education department, and she would often help chaperone at the volleyball games. My sister was a good volleyball player in high school and actually beginning her teaching and coaching career at that time, so this gave me an interest in the sport. Our volleyball team at Provo HS was excellent at that time, and I had some students that played on the team so I would often go to support. I thought she was cute, but I never knew that some of the staff members behind the scenes were plotting to get us together. I thought I had blown the opportunity as she came by my classroom to ask for a ride home. But I couldn't give her a ride home because I had to make it up to the state football playoff game. I was a sophomore football coach and I was expected to be there, though I didn't do much in the vein of coaching. Sometimes I was the "get back coach" or the coach assigned to keep the players from getting too close to the sidelines and in the designed players' box. If they got too close to the sidelines, you would tell them to "get back."

I did encourage her to come by next week if she needed a ride, I think her truck might have been in the shop or something. She did. We went on a date and hit it off. I took her to a nice Mexican restaurant in downtown Salt Lake called Cafe Pierpont and we went to the Jazz game. The Jazz would make the championship finals that year and lose to the Bulls. That night, they played the Houston Rockets led by

Charles Barkley. The Jazz actually lost that game but would knock the Rockets out with that famous shot by John Stockton in the playoffs.

The other memorable part of the date was when we were approached by a panhandler on our way back to my truck (I had one as well) who asked for some spare change. I didn't have any change and I think the lowest bill I had in my wallet was a five-dollar bill, so I just didn't know what to do. I thought the safe thing to do was be generous, I gave the guy five dollars. I found out that her favorite movie was the same as mine, "Casablanca", and watching that became our second date. Mom and Dad took an instant liking to her and through a friend at work, my Mom scored some tickets to *Hootie and the Blowfish,* our third official date.

I wasn't put in the friend zone and our romance blossomed, all while the wrestling season started. The wrestling season itself was very enjoyable and had many highlights and "my girl" Heidi along there with me. We set a school record (at that time) with 13 state qualifiers and state placers with eight and had three state finalists and one state champion. We beat our rival by a perfect 84-0 score to tie a national record for a dual meet, we had a comeback victory against our rival, a team we rarely beat over the years. We tied the defending 5A state champions in a dual meet 28-28 and won two invitational tournaments. We had one horrible setback as a team when we lost to the eventual state champions by one point in a dual meet. We were "robbed" in my humble opinion and my father was there to yell at the official and even his old coaching rival, who was the athletic director for the opposing school. And Heidi was there to comfort me in this defeat. But that 1996-97 wrestling season was a whirlwind for sure as was the entire school year, but mostly a good whirlwind.

One other important thing also happened that year which I think was the catalyst of good things to come. I decided to relocate to Provo. My father gave me some really sound advice. He saw how tired I was getting with commuting and trying to have a social life and do all the extracurricular things I was doing at the school. And he also felt I needed to become a part of the community in which I was teaching and coaching. And just maybe he knew some other things as well. I remembered one time he cornered me and he simply told me these words, "you need to move to Provo, good things will happen to you." But this meant I would now be an hour away from Mom and Dad instead of just a few minutes. This meant leaving Salt Lake, a city that I loved in many ways, a city much more diverse than Provo in many ways, a diversity I enjoyed and the one thing I felt was lacking at Provo High School when I compared it to West High School. This also meant leaving my Utah Jazz games, more fine dining choices and not seeing my friend Erik Holdaway as much.

But my father was right, I needed to move to Provo. After this decision is when I met my wife Heidi, but more importantly by being in Provo, we could have more time to be together. Our relationship progressed at a fast and furious pace. We were engaged in five weeks. But as I found out, "when you know, you know." It was an easy courtship that way and she really liked baseball and she really liked coming to the wrestling meets. But she had an artistic side and played the harp. I think about a month into our relationship that I spoke with the father of one of my top wrestlers, who was a jeweler, to get a ring. And after my wife played the harp in a Christmas program in downtown Provo at the old Tabernacle building, now a temple for the Church of Jesus Christ of Latter-day Saints, we found ourselves at my condo. I popped out the ring and proposed. I think it was December 16, but I couldn't wait for Christmas as she was a student at BYU and would be heading back to Colorado for Christmas or winter break. It seemed as good as time as any.

The 1996-97 school year at Provo High School was an amazing year in so many ways. We also won the baseball state title that year and it was fun to be a very tiny part of all that. Provo High also won state titles in boys' basketball and boys' track. And of course, the day the school year ended (on a Friday), I drove out with my roommate (and one of my assistant coaches) Tim Bird to marry my sweetheart the next day in Denver. We even stopped in Grand Junction so Tim could buy a lotto ticket and he hit enough numbers to win about 500 dollars. He could now pay his rent to me and hopefully, by the time our honeymoon was over, he could find a place to stay. But there was a bitter part of that school year and that was that six weeks before I got married my father had a stroke. Ten days later he would pass away. Heidi was graduating from BYU during all this time.

Again, not sure how I got through all of this. I remember his stroke happening late Sunday Night or early Monday morning. I missed a few days of school. He was supposed to die within 24 hours but my Dad is not one to "go gently into that good night." But then I decided to go back to work, go to baseball practice, and then drive up to the hospital. I would usually stay until late at night, sometimes Heidi would go with me. Again, she was taking her last finals, and she graduated on her birthday the day before my father would pass away. My father, one of the great's in coaching wrestling, passed away on a Friday night. The next Tuesday we had the funeral and then Heidi would go back to Broomfield, a small suburban town north of Denver, until our marriage date in late May. I remember how my Mom was a true rock in all of this. She is one really tough woman. I remember too, all my friends and fellow wrestlers stepping up to support me over this time, and all the people at Provo High School.

I remember all the people that came to the viewing, particularly my very first roommate, Chris Weston, from my BYU days, who I hadn't seen since my first year in college. But he was a wrestler and that's just what wrestlers do, we're there for each other. And my future in-laws Robert and Janet Stone were very supportive. But mostly, I thank Heidi for her love and support, and patience. It's not easy to see your future groom lose his father and coach a month before our nuptials. But she was there for me totally. I should also mention my uncle, Emery Schattinger, my Mom's brother who was my Dad's fraternity brother in college. He came with my Aunt Carol to support us for some time. I am so glad for them, my friends Darren and Erik, my assistant principal Steve Oliverson, and others like Cesar Cardoso, who was our Athletic Director , and other work colleagues like Jennifer Hyde (Young), Todd Smith, Margaret Craft, and Marge Hutchings. As well as my wrestlers and their parents. I can't thank them enough for them being there for me during this tough time. And when things got better for me a month later, many of these same people were there to celebrate my new venture of marriage.

CHAPTER SIX
SECOND CHANCE SUCCESSES

Dan Blanchard: Here we are in week seven of the wrestling season, and Dakota still hasn't wrestled a single day yet. I came out of a 15-year retirement from coaching to help coach him and his team, and I still haven't had a chance to coach him. Hopefully, I'm at least making a difference with his teammates. I know I'm enjoying it. We had a good practice today on this first day of the wrestling week. The wrestlers worked hard on the mat while Dakota worked hard off the mat on the bike. It seems like the positive attitude from this past weekend, where we wrestled well in Saturday's tournament, has carried over to today.

What I really liked about today, though, was the car ride home with Dakota, where we got to spend some time together talking. He told me that weight loss is coming easier for him now. I was happy to hear that because I know how miserable he was last year losing weight and how nervous he has been this year with just the thought of losing weight to make the 134-pound weight class.

I'm happy to hear his confidence in his ability to lose weight. It shows that he is maturing some. And now can do something challenging rather than just complain about it. And I'm sure that at some point during this season, he's going to tip the scale and he's going to have to suck it up without excuses to make weight for that day.

I also shared one of my secrets of success for wrestling with Dakota on the drive home tonight. I told him never to let himself get out of shape. Always, year-round, be in shape and have low body fat. One should never walk into the first wrestling practice of the season being out of shape and having to lose double digits to get back down to one's ideal wrestling weight.

Also, Dakota shared a little psychological trick with me that he has been using that reminds me of my own elders' council trick. My strategy consists of imagining that I have a council of older, wiser people to ask for advice when I run into a tight spot. I ask them what to do. Imagine a well-thought-out answer. And then go do that.

Dakota calls his trick the National Champion trick. He imagines what a national champion would do in a particular situation that he finds himself in. Then he does what he thinks a national champion would do. For example, would a national champion complain about an injury or just do the work to get healthy and strong again? Would a national champion complain about his body weight, or just do the work to make weight? I think we all know what a national champion would do, right?

So, in this vein, Dakota tells me that even though he's injured, he is doing as a national champion and trying to make the best use of his time. He's keeping his head up. Dakota is watching and studying lots of videos on wrestling. He's also helping other wrestlers with technique and mental toughness. And he's working out, even though it's just on a bike... Pretty cool, huh?

Tuesday's practice was pretty typical except for the fact that one of the up-and-coming new guys wasn't there. He skipped practice because his body is sore in a bunch of places. He believes that Coach wasn't fully listening to him yesterday when Coach told him, "You're not injured, you're just sore. So, get back out on the mat and keep wrestling."

This wrestler was seen walking the hallways today with his girlfriend during practice time. I can't imagine that head coach Torres is going to take this lightly.

This whole situation with this first-year wrestler is bumming me out because this kid has potential. But his immaturity might have just shot him in the foot. And he may never get the chance now to develop into the wrestler or young man that he could have been.

While walking out of the school building on Tuesday after practice, I share with Dakota how this whole situation of his teammate missing practice stinks. There needs to be a consequence. However, that consequence, and the boy's possible reactions to it, could end the season or even the wrestling career for this freshman.

I also share with Dakota that if there is one thing I know to be true after all these years, it's that potential doesn't equal greatness. I've seen a lot of wasted and unused potential over the years. Wrestling is a tough sport, and many kids don't make it. I've always said, "Anyone can wrestle, but it isn't for everyone."

Before school on Wednesday morning, I watched Dakota step onto our bathroom scale and saw the digits finally settle on 136. Dakota was shocked. He couldn't believe it. He finally spoke in disbelief, "How's that possible? How can I be two pounds overweight? I barely ate anything last night!"

With school all day and Dakota's limited ability to work out, making weight tonight for our match against RHAM will be tough for him. Even though he isn't wrestling tonight, Coach Torres wants Dakota to weigh in to establish a pattern of him making weight for the team's matches. Coach Torres is going to be pretty mad if Dakota doesn't make weight. Hopefully, Dakota doesn't forget to consult with his imaginary national champion on this one who we all know wouldn't complain and wouldn't make excuses. But instead, I would just find a way to man-up and get the job done...

Dakota got in a short workout after school today but was still a half-pound over when he boarded the team's bus for RHAM. He then proceeded to do something that doesn't shock anyone in the amateur wrestling world but horrifies people outside of it. And it especially grossed out his mom.

Dakota asked his mom for a piece of gum so he could spit off some weight on the bus ride. Coach Torres didn't think Dakota could spit off a whole half-pound on the ride. I shared that I've only seen kids spit off a quarter of a pound on short bus rides. It doesn't look like Dakota is going to make weight tonight. But Dakota doesn't seem worried about it. He even says, "Don't worry. I'll make it."

Breathes were held when Dakota finally stepped on the scale at RHAM. Everyone had made weight so far. Would Dakota be the first wrestler that night not to make weight? The scale's numbers flashed up and down for a bit and then finally settled on 133.8. He made weight somehow. None of us knew how he spit off seven-tenths of a pound on a short bus ride over. The RHAM coach, Ryan Fitch, looked a bit confused. He asked Dakota if he was wrestling because he knows from my blog that Dakota has been injured and is still recovering from surgery.

Dakota shook his head back and forth sideways and told Coach Fitch that he was just weighing in... And I'm sure only weighing in has a lot of us a bit confused. Sometimes, even Dakota wants to know if he has to make weight or just be close since he's not wrestling yet. The answer is pretty complicated and lengthy, so Coach usually just says, "make weight."

RHAM has a history of being well coached and having a strong program throughout the years with Kevin Kaniatis and now Ryan Fitch as their head coaches over the last couple of decades. Both are former East Hartford boys who, just like me, wrestled for East Hartford High School under the big, rough, and tough coach Steve Konopka.

Our team was determined that we were going to battle hard tonight and make a good showing even though they vastly outnumbered us in wrestlers and years of experience. And many of our wrestlers did indeed step up and wrestle tough tonight, but we still came up 12 points short. So close... That point spread could have been as little as just one of our wrestlers pinning his opponent instead of getting pinned. That one little thing would have caused the score to have been all tied up. So close... but no cigar... Regardless, our kids wrestled tough, and we're proud of them.

Hey! Guess what? Our freshman wrestler with potential is back. Coach benched him for one day, not allowing him to travel on the team bus to Wednesday's match, and he took the consequence like a man and showed up ready to work hard on Thursday. I'm thrilled that this turned out well. The coach had a measured action, and the boy didn't overreact to correction from his coach. This is a good thing. And now we can get back to helping this young boy become a good young man someday.

Thursday and Friday's practices went pretty well. However, Coach Torres didn't think the kids had enough pep in their step. So, he gave them a bunch of extra conditioning to wake them up and get them moving. I tell you, I wish I could still move like these young athletic kids, even when they are not moving at their fastest. I ran sprints with them at the end of practice and came in dead last every time. This hurts a little bit because I still remember how I used to always come in first. But I guess, just like everyone else, I need to stop and count my blessings on what I have, rather than grumbling over what I don't have. Just a couple of months ago, I couldn't even run because of a hip replacement surgery I had that has sidelined me for the last decade. So, the fact that I am running now is really a blessing and even a victory in itself even at a much slower pace.

In Friday's practice, I had an understandable but frustrating moment when I was trying to coach a kid who was tired and frustrated himself. I was on him about keeping his head up and being in a good position during a particular drill we were doing. And eventually, he turned and looked at me, and politely said, "It's just a drill."

I knew the kid was tired and frustrated. So I just gently reminded him that in matches, he was going to be tired there too. And he would do the same exact thing there that he is doing here by dipping his head. Again, he politely declined my help by repeating, "It's just a drill."

I gave him the look that I knew he was better than that. And I will follow up on this later on at a better time when he isn't tired and frustrated. Hopefully, at a later time, he will be more receptive and be more coachable.

You see, being coachable is one of the keys to success and becoming a good man. One of the challenges this young boy is going to have though is that he's already a pretty good wrestler and has already had some success even though he dips his head and is not always in the best position. Sometimes good can be the enemy of great. And suppose one is already doing pretty well. In that case, they don't always find it necessary to change anything that they are presently doing.

I know here in the United States, we pride ourselves on cutting our own path. But the bottom line is that after working with thousands and thousands of kids over multiple decades, the most successful ones are the ones that are personable, (have social skills), hungry to learn more than what they already know, and are coachable.

Sometimes I wish I could just pour the knowledge and skills that I have into young people's heads so they can be wildly successful through knowing what I know. This would help them avoid a lot of the pitfalls and pain of growing up. But unfortunately, the world doesn't work that way. And if it was possible, our young people would probably just decline it anyway. They would probably think that that is too weird, and they want to do it their own way. We call this stubbornness. They call it independence.

In thinking a little more about this… Our Creator does works in mysterious ways, though…. So, I suppose if our older generation really could just simply pour our knowledge and skills into the next generation, making them younger versions of ourselves, then it really wouldn't be fair to the older generation. After all, the older generations had to go through many ups and downs, bumps and bruises, exhilaration, and tears to get to where we are now. I guess there are no shortcuts for our youth. They, too, have to go through the hard times and good times, just like we did, so they also can toughen up, build character through experience, and become good young men and women, too, someday who cut their own paths.

Saturday arrived, and so did a snowstorm that postponed our Saturday tournament. The regular world may like this day off from being snowed in, but not the wrestlers. This means the wrestling tournament is on Sunday this week, instead of Saturday. It also means that the wrestlers have an additional day of sacrificing to make weight, and their one day off this week is gone. This is more sacrifice for the wrestlers that most civilians aren't even aware of as they eat, sip hot chocolate, and peer out the window at their beautiful winter wonderland.

Oh, well… These are the kinds of things that make and forges a good young man, right? Now it's time to watch our weight and get in a workout or two through shoveling. No snow blowers allowed! Only man-power…

Sunday's tournament was tough. We ran into a lot of good kids who gave us a real hard time. We just didn't have a pep in our step today. I don't know if it was the snow day off yesterday, or was the competition just that tough today. It was another very long day where we left in the dark and came home in the dark, and all we had to show for it was a second-place and two third-place medals. I know… that's better than nothing… but it just seemed like one of those days today where we went through the motions and couldn't catch any breaks… Oh well… there's always tomorrow, I guess. We'll be coming right back to this same school tomorrow for the jayvee tournament. I am feeling good about our chances to win some medals tomorrow.

Also, I want to share another wrestler's poem I ran across today. It's called, "He Stands Alone."

He Stands Alone

What high school sport makes the demands on the individual that amateur wrestling does? When a boy walks onto the mat, he stands alone. No one will run interference, no one will pass him the ball when he is under the net, and no one will catch a high fly if he makes a bad pitch. He stands alone. In other high school sports, where individual scores are kept, the contest is determined in time, distance, and height. But in wrestling, the score is kept on a boy's ability to overcome an opponent in a hand to hand contest, where a two-second interval at any time can mean a loss or a win. If an opponent gains an advantage, there will be no help, no substitute; there will be no time out, and all can be lost in two seconds. Yes, the boy stands alone.

There is no place on a wrestling team for the show-off, the halfhearted, or the weakling. When the whistle blows, a boy puts his ability, his determination, and his courage on the line.

We who are close to the young men on our high school wrestling teams, have watched the range of human emotions from elation to heartbreak.

We have seen coaches with tears running down their cheeks as they try to console a young man who has given his all. Yet lost.

Wrestling is a tough, hard sport, a life where it is the survival of the fittest. The young men who enter and stay with the team know this. They also know that when the time comes and the whistle blows...

They Stand Alone!

Brian Preece: As I read Daniel's writing I thought about the one young man who had missed practice because he was sore and was out in the hallway with a girl during practice. I think many coaches in what we might call the major sports like baseball, basketball, or football would have kicked the kid right off the team. Maybe if the kid was a star player some might show a bit of patience for that indiscretion. But for wrestling coaches and coaches of individual sports like track or cross-country, it might not be that simple. And if you're a struggling football program, it might not even be that simple. Coaches in sports where they are having some amount of success have excess athletes or depth on their teams and prospective athletes to choose from, sometimes it is easier to either get on their moral platitudes or just be stricter with the rules. But at the same time, I'm also reminded of that one quote or saying often attributed to Super Bowl-winning coach Bill Parcells of the New York Giants, "you get what you tolerate."

So finding the right balance and the right way to message (or the right messenger) is sometimes key to getting an athlete or prospective athlete to step up. And I generally think when you are building a wrestling program, some amount of understanding as a coach is necessary. You can't expect your athletes to have the same motivation as you or even the same motivation as your assistant coaches and top athletes in your program. I think you have to be patient, encourage them, and then find the right time to appropriately challenge them. And sometimes that challenge might have to come from many fronts.

Case in point. In my second year as a head coach at Provo High School, we had a young man join our team as a junior. He had a lot of talent and some experience as a youth wrestler. I remember coaching his older brother when I was a college intern. His brother tragically passed away and of course, it had a huge impact on this young man. I was glad to have him on the team but his commitment to the sport and team wasn't the best at first. One thing that was hard was that he was definitely a varsity caliber wrestler, but we had two excellent wrestlers in the weight classes around his weight. He weighed about 200 pounds at this time. But we didn't have a 285-pounder, so he stepped in for us at that weight class as a very light heavyweight.

We had a Saturday tournament and he was a no-show. I think we ended up taking third or fourth in that tournament and coming in second was well within reach if he would have come and wrestled to his usual level. And coming home with a trophy would have been nice for a program that was trying to reach the next level. But what was even more infuriating was that when our bus arrived back at the school close to 11:00 p.m., there was a stomp (or informal school dance) finishing up in the main gym. And there he was. I did catch his eye, and I was fuming inside but I said nothing, went into my coach's office, and did what I needed to do to get the other boys home and me as well. I was still living up in Salt Lake, and we had a winter storm that day and I wasn't looking forward to the hour or so driving back home.

Well, Monday practice rolled around and he strolled in as nothing had happened. But what was nice was somebody on the team said something to him like, "We really could have used you." And a couple of others even joked about his dance moves but in a way that said, "What you did (or didn't do) wasn't cool." I think that reached his soul a bit. First, when one of our team captains said, "We could have really used you." it sent a message that not just his coaches wanted him there, but they wanted him there and he would have made a difference in the team race. And his choice of activities versus what his teammates were doing, just wasn't cool.

I really wanted to blow up at him and maybe even kick him off the team. It wasn't the first time he missed a team function, and I had to say I was losing my patience. And I was wondering what message I was sending the other athletes. But again, I think with some sports or situations, more patience or understanding or whatever is needed. And I felt he really needed wrestling for his personal growth.

As practice progressed, to his credit, he apologized to me for missing the meet. I didn't exactly say, "it was alright and all was forgiven," but I just challenged him to step up. And I laid the guilt on him a bit by telling him that he cost us winning a trophy, and that would have meant a lot to our program, his coaches, and his teammates. I thought he could handle it and I felt he knew that as coaches we really cared about him. And stepped up he did. He placed sixth in the state after winning region (or league) for us that year, but I remember one match in particular at State where he was outweighed by nearly 85 pounds and fought off being pinned for nearly the entire second round and came back to win the match by one point to go to the semifinals.

The next year he became one of our team leaders and took third in the state losing in the semifinals in a heartbreaker, which is a story in itself. But he also got two big pins in our dual meets, one to help us tie the returning state champion team from the larger-school classification, and then propelling us to a come-from-behind victory against one of our league rivals. And one time he lost in a dual meet to a defending state champion but his loss led to our overall victory. It was a dual meet tournament and both teams were undefeated and it was coming down to the last match in the last dual meet of the tournament. They were down to us by four points and they just felt their stud would just go pin our undersized 285-pounder and they would win the meet by two points. But our guy battled and lost by three or four points and we won the dual by one point along with the tournament.

So I thought holding my tongue and controlling my own anger served me well, and this young man well. So my thoughts I might have for Daniel and Coach Torres is to maybe be patient and maybe have the teammates challenge this young man to step up. Tell him that they want him to be part of the team. I know sometimes the right message from the right messenger(s) can go further, especially if it comes from a peer group.

And pondering about this young man, and this particular group of wrestlers I coached, made me think of another situation with a different young man on this team. And the peer groups weren't even wrestlers but just really good friends supporting their friend, a wrestler. After we got that 28-28 tie against the returning 5A state champions, one of our wrestlers did win by seven points. But he was leading by 10 or 11 points at one point, and the key thing is that if you win by eight points you secure a major decision and another point for your team. That would have been the difference in winning or tying that dual meet.

A few of his friends were there watching the meet, and I know a couple of them were on our very highly successful basketball team that would end up taking state that year. I never knew about this until he became an assistant coach for me and told this story to our wrestlers. But when he was about ready to catch a ride with his friends, they told him "go get your workout stuff, you're not riding in the car with us. You're out of shape and that's why you let that kid come back on you and you didn't win by enough points. You're going to run home and we'll ride by you all the way home." Well, I'm not sure that was the exact quote but close enough. These were some good friends. They didn't do it to be mean, they just wanted their friend to have success like they were having in basketball. By way, he also ended up taking third in the state that year after taking second in the region.

And I must say this, I loved our basketball teams in this era, as they were some great boys and athletes. And of course, our basketball coach could safely say if you miss a game or practice, you could find something else to do. But I also appreciated that many of them came to support our wrestlers. And they set a great example of hard work and commitment.

I know sometimes there can be friction between basketball and wrestling programs, and I'm not saying there wasn't some between ours at times, but to me, they were a model of success. But I also knew that I had to do some things differently. I didn't have 15 spots on my team and maybe hundreds of others that would give anything to be on the team. I had a lot of athletes that were investigating the sport, trying to figure out if this was something that they wanted to do. And wrestling is a tough sport in a lot of ways from the workouts to the nature of the competition where it's a true one-on-one sport and losing is a bit harder on the athlete. So sometimes you just need to have a bit more patience and understanding and then appropriately challenge at that right time with the right people. Then hopefully they will step up to the plate and make that stronger commitment.

CHAPTER SEVEN
TOURNAMENT AND SEEDING MEETING FUN

Dan Blanchard: This week started a bit different. Monday is Martin Luther King Jr.'s birthday, so we don't have any school today. But, what we do have is a 6:45 a.m. bus to a jayvee wrestling tournament back in Griswold. It's the same place we were yesterday for the varsity tournament. It's the second day in a row that we are on a bus in the dark of the morning and then again in the darkness of the night. And in between all the traveling, we're yelling ourselves hoarse in a very crowded gymnasium. It's another long, exhausting day of wrestling, just like yesterday.

We only brought with us eight wrestlers today. And while they all wrestled tough, it was our 113-pounder that really stood out. He fought four very tough opponents, and he somehow managed to squeak out wins in all of them. Thus, landing himself on the top step of the awards podium at the end of the night. We are all so proud of this first-year wrestler taking first place in this tournament. He's innately tough, and he has a bright future as a wrestler.

A couple of other cool things also happened today at the tournament. A mother approached me and told me that she and her son had read my book, *The Storm: How Young Men Become Good Men.* That was very cool! I also received a phone call from Ernie Hutt of

Augie and Ray's restaurant in East Hartford to discuss an East Hartford football book that I'm in the process of writing. And to top it off, my old buddy Tim Victor called me, too. Tim lives in Philadelphia now, but back in 1987, he was my teammate and the captain of what many call the best East Hartford wrestling team ever. Tim and I are collaborating on an East Hartford wrestling alumni project that could involve some kind of wrestling book.

Above are some of the good things that happened today. The bad thing is that my son Dakota complained yesterday that his knee felt weird, and now today, it's feeling even worse. I could see on his face that he's worried. His frustration pains me even more than the thought that maybe he won't make it back for the State Tournament this year… Perhaps this season is a wash for Dakota… I hope not… Sitting on the sideline this season with a knee that won't heal fast enough has been tough on Dakota.

Surprisingly, my old Junior Olympic teammate from the mid-80s, Rey Santiago, showed up later in the day to help referee the tournament. After the Junior Olympics, Rey wrestled on the Pan Am Team with another old buddy and teammate out of Hartford, Orlando Rosa, and a guy from Massachusetts named Jose Santiago. The three did well and earned a bunch of medals there. They were invited to be on the Puerto Rico Olympic wrestling team to compete in the 1996 Olympics in Atlanta, Georgia. Of course, I went to watch because I didn't yet have all the responsibilities of raising a family while holding down a demanding job yet. Also, all my money was still my own back then, too. So, I could still spend some on myself back then.

I introduced our Coach Scot Rogers to Rey Santiago. I figured they'd have a lot to talk about. Orlando Rosa was Coach Rogers' arch-rival back in his old high school days. The three of us had a great stroll down memory lane talking about the old days of wrestling. As I, Coach Rogers, and Rey Santiago were talking, laughing, and joking over the old days, we had sort of noticed that wrestling had stopped. But because we were so deep into memories, we just kept talking. We didn't see that wrestling had stopped because of us three old warriors trading stories while standing on the wrestling mat in use. When it was finally brought to our attention, Rogers and I got off the mat, and Rey made a joke about how it was all my fault. And then he ran out to the center of the mat to finally referee the match that had been patiently waiting for him to arrive.

I settled back into the bleachers to watch some more wrestling when a mother asked me what a "Bye" was. I tried to explain that it was a free pass to the next round for a wrestler. She asked me if it was a forfeit.

"Not exactly," I told her. "It's a bit different."

She asked me if it was a form of "by." I wasn't sure, so I looked it up.

The first thing we found out was that the term is not related to "goodbye" but is indeed an alteration of "by" as in the team or athlete is "standing by" to play later or "bypassed" while other teams or athletes play now. One of the earliest sports to feature a bye is coursing, where animals, usually dogs, pursue some kind of game animal, like a rabbit. We also found out that the b-y-e spelling is likely influenced by an existing term from cricket in which a wicket-keeper misses a ball. Wow. What a history here in sports that I wasn't even aware of until some curious mom asked me an innocent question.

When I arrived at practice on Tuesday, I saw Dakota, and he tells me that his physical therapy session didn't go so well. There is definitely something weird going on with his knee again. His physical therapist only wants Dakota doing core work today. He's to stay off of his feet and do a bunch of sit-ups, crunches, flutter kicks, and things like that. Coach Torres doesn't look happy upon being informed of this new development.

Dakota looks at me and says, "How am I supposed to make weight tomorrow for a match I'm not even going to wrestle?

I reply, "You may not be making weight tomorrow," which was reinforced when Dakota stepped on the scale at the end of practice at 138-pounds. He's four pounds over after his core workout. Dakota weighing-in tomorrow doesn't look good. Another obstacle has been thrown in his path to wrestling at all this season…

Wednesday night was quite a night. Dakota didn't make weight. And our 120-pounder didn't make weight either. He missed it by one-tenth of a pound. Thus, Coach bumped him up two weight classes to the next open weight class of 134-pounds. This is the weight class Dakota would have wrestled in if he was healthy and on weight. Sadly, their 134-pounder was awesome, and he just overwhelmed our 120-pound first-year wrestler.

As one can probably guess, the night brought with it some good stuff and some bad stuff once again. It was good because I got to go to the wrestling meet with my wife, Jennifer, and she got to watch the team wrestle tonight. It was also good because I got to see my old buddy and former teammate, Paul Diaz, too. Paul is the assistant coach of Enfield's wrestling program. He introduced me to his son, who, like my son, has had to weather an injury as well. It was great seeing and talking to the old heavyweight of my 1988 East Hartford High School team. It was also great to see Enfield fan and father, Scott Beiler. We've met and talked a few times earlier this season about my blog and are now friends. Pretty cool, huh?

Also, tonight's referee is a guy that used to referee some of mine and Coach Rogers, and even Coach Torres' matches when we were high school wrestlers. Mr. Kelly Murphy has been refereeing since 1982. He told me that he used to love to referee those very physical matches that Steve Konopka's East Hartford teams used to have back during my era against our rival Manchester coached by Barry Bernstein. Murphy said those matches were very rough, tough, and exciting. I was there on those mats in the middle of it all, and I agree.

In addition, our 138-pound senior captain had a good night by dominating and pinning his opponent. Our 160-pound sophomore went up against a tough Enfield boy and pulled out a victory by pinning him in a far-side half-nelson. We bumped up our 182-pound junior to the next weight class of 195-pounds, and he went out there with both guns blazing and pinned his kid in under 30 seconds. I call him my brawler. He's my throwback to the old rough and tough days. And he's really fun to watch.

Unfortunately, the rest of our team was just outmatched tonight. The Enfield team was strong, and they showed it on the mat in just about every weight class. Coach Flynn, Coach Diaz, and the other Enfield coaches are doing a great job with their wrestling program.

They also have a strong wrestling youth program in Enfield. Unfortunately, we don't even have a youth program. Hey, good for them. Not so good for us... It was pretty much a painful night for most of us E.O. Panther parents.

Hey, our coaching staff consists of two coaches from Windham, Torres, and Rogers. And myself from East Hartford. We grew up very different from the kind of kid that we are coaching today. Windham has a long history of being a powerhouse wrestling program. They own ten state championship titles. Windham is also a rough and tough town. If a Windham kid comes up against another kid who has more experience and technique than them, it doesn't mean they were automatically beat. The Windham boys bring a rough style street-fighting instinct to the match where there surely will be a battle. And because of that sure-to-be battle, the Windham boys always have a chance of somehow winning.

Myself, being from East Hartford, well, while we don't have a history of ten state championships like Windham, we're similar in many ways. Every kid we went against was surely going to know he was in a battle and was looking at that clock to hurry and finish up those six minutes.

I think Coach Torres and Coach Rogers knew that Enfield had us outmatched before we even began. So, I believe they wanted our kids to take it to the next level of physicality. The coaches wanted the Enfield boys to know they were in one heck of a fight. But, we didn't see that street-level toughness out of our boys tonight. And it's not very surprising since it's different times. Our boys' hometown is a very different place from where their coaches had grown up.

Regardless, Coach Torres wasn't going to let this one go. Thursday was our hardest practice of the season. It reminded me of the old days. Torres had a fire in his eyes, and he pushed our boys to the brink where I thought some of them would break down and cry, or at least quit. They made a lot of noise grunting, but no one cried, and every one of them showed up again the next day for practice. I'm proud of the boys!

During Friday's practice, Coach Torres was back to his old self, wearing that million-dollar smile again. Today's workout was a good practice that even consisted of a little smiling and laughing. The kids worked hard and seemed to be really interested in learning all they could. At one point during the practice, Dakota got off the bike and said, "Hey, dad, I want to show you a cross-face." He then proceeded to nearly rip my face off.

"Dang!" I said. "How did you do that? I've never been hit with a cross-face like that before!" It sort of reminded me of the grueling tight-waist he showed me last week that no one has ever done to me either. Hmm... I wish I could have seen him wrestle this year. He has some excellent stuff, and he's tough, too. I wonder how he would have done against Enfield's stud, who was in his 134-pound weight class...

Other bright points of Friday's practice were when I showed our 160-pounder how to drag out of being on the bottom in a chicken-wing, and our 182-pounder came over and said, "Hey, that's a really cool move. Can you show it again?" I also pulled aside our 138-pound captain, who has had a nearly flawless season this year, and showed him how I think he can improve his chances of scoring when he shoots with some quick drags, and a very cool 1980s dump that I used to beat the heck out of kids. Surprisingly, nobody is really using that old dump anymore. And as I suspected, our senior captain had never seen that dump before. He loved it. Look out, other 138-pounders out there, our captain just learned another way to score on you.

Friday's practice ended, and so did our week. We don't have a meet tomorrow. Our boys were ordered to do some running on their own, get to bed early, lay off the food, and study for their final exams. And, of course, be good young men. Naturally, I don't have the day off. I have a couple of very early morning meetings I need to get to, followed by a long day of soccer games for my daughters, which I will repeat on Sunday, too. Sometimes I feel like the Beatles when they used to sing that song, *Eight Days a Week...*

Brian Preece: When Daniel was trying to explain the difference between a "bye" and a "forfeit" in wrestling, it got me thinking of some crazy seeding meetings I have been to over the years.

A seeding meeting is where the coaches meet to decide where to place the wrestlers on the bracket with the idea of the most deserving wrestlers getting the best seeds and therefore increasing the chances that the two best wrestlers meet in the championship finals and the best overall wrestlers place in the tournament. But seeding meetings can be contentious. Now with Track Wrestling, the data it has can help with the process, but even then, there is always some contention.

The seeding meeting brings in all sorts of coaching personalities or quirks. There is always the one coach that is disorganized, has no records of anything. It's not that their teams aren't good, they often are, and that sometimes makes the whole situation even more aggravating. Trying to find out if their wrestler beat or lost to someone is much like using the Rosetta Stone to decipher Egyptian hieroglyphics, somewhere between difficult but doable and impossible.

Then there's the coach that has all the records and is there to correct anyone that makes any mistake. He even knows who your wrestlers competed against better than you do. There are the quiet coaches, there are the argumentative coaches, they're the coaches that just like to eat and shoot the breeze and only worry about their better wrestlers getting the best seeds. And of course, you have your manipulators that will use any quirk in criteria to their advantage whether their wrestler deserves it or not.

I would like to think I knew my stuff, I knew where to put my wrestlers on the bracket to maximize their chances, and could argue as needed with the best of them. I guess I was the one guy that coaches often trusted for correct information, so I guess I was a bit like the guy that had all the information. But I usually didn't speak up until asked or if it benefitted my wrestlers. My Dad, on the other hand, was known for being loud, argumentative, and so forth at seeding meetings. He really fought for his kids and some coaches claimed he got better seeds than what his wrestlers sometimes deserved. But he also told me there were times to shut up and take the lower seed because it would be better for your wrestler in the end. Sometimes the sixth seed is better than the fourth seed because that will put you away from the number one seed, and if your wrestler from the sixth seed is good enough to pull off an upset or two, it will pay off.

The seeding meeting also became complicated in Utah about 25 years ago when we first decided to let two wrestlers from each team wrestle in the qualifying region tournaments. So how we looked at "jayvee" wrestlers was interesting. Over time, things have got a bit clearer but at the start of things, it wasn't exactly clear on what to do and so forth. Oftentimes, for a good program, the jayvee or second-string wrestler is almost as good as the varsity wrestler and would beat the varsity wrestlers of other schools if given the opportunity. Now in Utah, most good programs will send their jayvee wrestlers to varsity tournaments, and with Track Wrestling, results can be more easily tracked and so forth.

The region or league I coached at decided one year to have a jayvee tournament and the top two wrestlers would qualify for the varsity tournament. We had six teams in our region so that would just complete the 8-wrestler bracket. And of course, the jayvee qualifiers would be the seventh and eighth seeds. But sometimes the jayvee wrestlers were so good they would often beat the number two seed and the whole bracket was thrown into chaos. Then it was decided to let each school just bring two wrestlers to the region tournament and a 16-wrestler bracket was used with some byes.

There was one seeding meeting I remember that got real contentious and one of the culprits was excessively strong personalities and unclear rules from our region handbook. There were a lot of coaching legends in this seeding meeting including Steve Sanderson, the father of Cael Sanderson, and Darold Henry, who was Steve Sanderson's coach, and one of the winningest coaches in Utah history. There was also my former high school and college coach Alan Albright, and there were other coaches, like me, that had been around long enough and weren't going to be pushed around.

We spent almost an hour before we even seeded a weight class just arguing over whether jayvee wrestlers should be seeded. Of course, the general rule for any seeding meeting is that coaches will act in their self-interest, or so they think. And there was one team that was favored to win the region (and the state) and they had a lot of good jayvee wrestlers that were often the second, third, or fourth-best wrestlers in the weight class. But it was finally decided to just throw the jayvee wrestler on the other side of the bracket from their varsity wrestler. So in wrestling, the top-seeded and fourth-seeded wrestlers are on the "top" side of the bracket, so if your wrestler got those seeds, the jayvee wrestler would just go into the bottom part of the bracket somewhere, and not as a seed, as jayvee wrestlers were not to be seeded.

I found myself on the side of my old high school and college coach, where he was now an assistant coach on the team (Spanish Fork) favored to win the region title. My general mindset is to seed the wrestlers where they deserved to be seeded as it will just disrupt the bracket. I didn't win any friends when I said, "we all know what this is about, we're just out to screw Spanish Fork, but by screwing Spanish Fork, we're just going to screw ourselves when their jayvee wrestlers win matches against other seeded wrestlers in the first round of the tournament." Or something to that effect. And at the 215-pound class, I knew I had a dilemma.

During the season, I didn't have a 285-pound or heavyweight wrestler. But I had two very good 215-pounders. One placed second in the state the year before and the other one was an athletic kid coming into his own but still learning the sport a bit as a junior. So during dual meets, I wrestled my jayvee 215-pound wrestler in that weight as my varsity wrestler and had my stud wrestler go up and wrestle 285 pounds. But the intention at region and state was to put both in at the 215-pound weight class. My jayvee wrestler was undefeated at the weight class against varsity competition, and now according to the rules, he wouldn't get a seed at all. Now, he did well in region dual meets, but he wasn't so good that it was a sure lock he could knock off the better-seeded wrestlers. So I wanted him to have a seed. Of course, I brought up my arguments but the coaches rallied against me, except for the Spanish Fork coaches.

But that's when I threw a wrench into the works. I just said, give my jayvee wrestler the top seed, which I felt he earned, and just make my varsity guy the jayvee wrestler. At this point, I was called every name in the book. But I stuck to my guns, my jayvee wrestler went 6-0 in region duals and deserved the number one seed. I said, "He's my varsity wrestler." What was great was then the Spanish Fork coaches wanted to go back and reseed the other weights and do what I did, seed their jayvee wrestler (that did enough to earn a seed) and throw their varsity guys in on the other side of the bracket as jayvee wrestlers, but it was voted that weights already completed were done and would not be changed. (Let's just say this seeding meeting took well over three hours.)

So the varsity wrestler that took second in the state was just drawn in. I think we had seven teams in our region but byes are randomly drawn in so he was drawn into the number-two seed, who happened to be coached by one of my good friends, Lyle Mangum. To make matters even more complicated, it was also against the school where my own sister taught and coached. Let's just say Lyle was very upset with me. The seeding meeting was the night before the region tournament and I tossed and turned all night over the situation, maybe thinking I should reverse course in the morning. I talked with my assistant coaches and even my old high school coach and they told me I was right on two levels. I should give my own wrestlers the best chance of success, and that my argument that this system of "throwing jayvee wrestlers on the other side of the bracket without a seed if it was deserved" was absurd. Of course, my wrestler pinned his wrestler and sent his wrestler right off the bat to consolations.

It looked like I had some egg on my face when my jayvee wrestler, the top seed, got beat in the semifinals. A few of the coaches got in my face about it and I just said, "That's why I wanted him to have a seed, it wasn't a sure lock he would win or even place in this tournament if he was just 'thrown in' without a seed." And yes, my true varsity wrestler from the number-fifteen seeded position won the tournament easily and my jayvee wrestler ended up fourth. But I felt I was rectified in the end when my varsity wrestler ended up second in the state and my jayvee wrestler ended up fifth in the state, and we were the only two state placers from our region. I just knew in my heart that my wrestlers were the two best wrestlers from our region and should have been seeded that way.

As it turned out, what I did made some waves across the state and I had more people on my side than I thought. And over time my position is the position we now use in seeding jayvee wrestlers. Every team can bring two wrestlers to their region or divisional qualifying tournament and they will be seeded based on their varsity record like any other wrestler. And as I have alluded to, many of the top programs get their jayvee and even their third and fourth string wrestlers matches against varsity competition. In fact, our top large-school program Pleasant Grove will usually compete in three varsity tournaments every weekend. And for the teams that can't do that, they will just put their top-level jayvee wrestlers in the varsity tournament or wrestle them in dual meets against weaker varsity wrestlers when possible to get those wins and seeding criteria to their favor.

I think allowing jayvee wrestlers a chance to go to State has really helped the quality of competition in our state and really helped our numbers. But when we did this some 25 years ago, it wasn't an easy process figuring out what to do. I had an idea of what we should do. But thanks again to time, experience, my persuasive arguments (ha ha), and Track Wrestling, seeding wrestlers, including jayvee wrestlers competing in varsity competitions, has got a lot simpler. And I do wish in Connecticut that they would allow jayvee wrestlers a chance to compete at state, so Dakota didn't feel like he needed to cut so much weight to make the varsity line-up.

CHAPTER EIGHT

WHAT'S NEXT AS COVID-19 HITS AMERICAN SHORES?

Dan Blanchard: It's Monday again. And guess what? I missed wrestling practice today. Near the end of my workday of teaching, I got a call from my wife. She and my daughter were at an urgent care center. They were being sent to the Connecticut Children's Hospital in Hartford. The doctors were very concerned with what was going on with my daughter.

My wife let me know that a family friend had agreed to drive Dakota to wrestling practice and then come back a few hours later to pick him up. My wife's sister took our other daughters to her house and then to their soccer practices. Thank goodness for family and friends.

I texted Coach Torres and Coach Rogers to let them know that I wouldn't be at practice tonight. I hate missing wrestling practice. I hate not being there to help the team out. But, in a situation like this, family comes first. Coach Torres and Coach Rogers were nothing but supportive. They told me to go be with my little girl in her time of need.

It was a very long and exhausting day and night in the hospital overrun with patients who had the same flu-like virus that my daughter was diagnosed with. I wondered if I was seeing an outbreak of this new thing called COVID-19, and they either weren't telling us or didn't know. Thankfully, we were now back home. And we were very thankful to be watching our much-improved daughter sleeping in her own bed. Wrestling and Dakota will have to wait until tomorrow.

Tomorrow is here, and so is wrestling again. The practice went well. The atmosphere felt light and kind of fun. Dakota was up and down from the stationary exercise bike, mixing in some pedaling, calisthenics, and some tips he shared with teammates on technique.

Dakota tells me that he feels that his knee is getting better, but he still can't bend it all the way. And that has both of us a bit concerned.

Practice finishes up with some sprints that I feel lucky to participate in, even if I am still coming in last for now. Eventually, I won't be last anymore. Coach Torres also jumps in to run sprints with the boys, and practice ends on a pretty good note. One of our upper-weights even slapped me on the back and said, "Good job, Coach." Pretty cool, huh?

Everything seems to be good except for Dakota. He is still three pounds over for tomorrow's weigh-in. We're wrestling East Catholic. Unfortunately, once again, Dakota won't be wrestling. On his face, I can see that he is frustrated with the strenuous efforts it takes to make weight and how it's even harder now when he's not even wrestling tomorrow. Boy, I tell you, if someone wants to test what they're made of by doing something hard and frustrating, wrestling is definitely something one should try.

On a positive note, I've dropped about five pounds a month over these first two months of wrestling season so far, equaling a ten-pound loss. My clothes are fitting a little bit better again, and I'm hoping I can continue this trend into and through the third and last month of this wrestling. So, in contrast to my son Dakota, who hates losing weight, I'm kind of enjoying losing some weight. Thanks, wrestling...

I noticed some daylight today for the first time this season as my wife and I are pulling up to the high school for our weekly Wednesday wrestling meet. It's just a bit after five o'clock. And I'm drawn back to when I was a kid wrestling and last season when I was in my garage putting on my shoes for the East Catholic match when I also saw some light coming through the window. The visible daylight reminded me back then like it did when I was a kid, as it does also on this Wednesday night that this season is winding down. We only have about three weeks left.

East Catholic, which was the first team I ever coached, way back when I was just 20 years old, is dealing with the illness that is going around that has sidelined four of their wrestlers. Tonight's meet is at home, which is a good thing for us because some of our home fans get to watch us wrestle. We wrestled well from the beginning to the end tonight and supplied our fans with a hometown victory.

Once again, our first-year 113-pound wrestler wrestled tough tonight. He won two matches convincingly against decent opponents. He's having a first-year wrestler dream season. Some of our less experienced guys also pulled off big wins tonight. So, everyone is happy. For our last match of the night, our 120-pound jayvee wrestler used a move I showed him, and he pinned his kid, capping off the night on a high note. He came off the mat and high-fived me. But, he missed my hand and jammed my thumb. Thus, causing the smile to run away from my face, replaced by a grimace of pain.

As I turned to look at our pumped-up team while holding my thumb, I thought about how crazy it is to be reminded that one could get hurt at any time in this sport, even if they're not wrestling. As I'm reflecting and nursing my thumb, I see my son Dakota, who still hasn't wrestled a single day this season yet, and I think about how I can feel his pain. And it really hurts, especially right now, in my thumb and heart. I hope my thumb and Dakota are okay soon...

Well, it turns out that I didn't need my thumb this Thursday except for the power-point clicker I'm using at the speech I'm delivering to the American Federation of teachers. I can't believe this, but I'm missing a second practice this week. However, this speech was scheduled way before the wrestling season began. And people are expecting me to be there and deliver a speech that makes it worth their time to be there, too.

I'm psyched! The speech went well, and I was hired on the spot for two more speeches from people out of the audience. And even better is what happened next. When I got home, I went to Dakota's bedroom to ask him how wrestling went today, and he told me that his knee is feeling better and better and can almost bend it all the way now. He even showed me how he can now get into the referee position, which he couldn't do before. My mind begins racing that maybe this season isn't a wash. How cool would it be if Dakota came back for the State Tournament and actually placed in it...? Yeah... against all odds... placed in the States... Hmm...

Dang... now I have that terrible cold that's been whipping around here and nailing everyone in its path. Friday at work was a long day. However, I did make it to wrestling practice today. But decided not to dress and coach from afar so I wouldn't get any of the kids sick. As I arrived at practice, I can already see that about half of the team is already ill or still ill. Dang again... Tomorrow is going to be a long day...

However, on a good note, Dakota comes over, and we do a father-son hug like we always do. The female wrestling managers collectively give an, "Ahh... that's so cute..." I smile and enjoy the moment because I know that it is something special that Dakota and I have. He also tells me that physical therapy went well today. He can now bend his knee enough and shows me how he can get into the referee position again. Cool. Very cool. Coach Torres and I begin immediately strategizing how we can get him back into the lineup for the upcoming State Tournament, or even sooner.

Saturday morning Dakota and I are pulling up to the high school in the dark once again to catch our 6:00 a.m. bus. As we're pulling into the parking lot, I discuss with Dakota how someday he may be the senior captain of this team. And on how days like this, he needs to show real leadership by being the first wrestler here and the last to leave. And then, if he ever becomes a coach, he needs to be the first person there and the last one to leave as well. Heck, I even revert back to my old army days and how the leader was the last one to eat. He needs to assure that all of his men have eaten and been taking care of first before he eats... Maybe it was a little over the top, but that's what I learned in the military, and I still believe that that's good leadership. One always takes care of their men first and leads by example.

Dakota didn't make weight today. He missed it by a few tenths of a pound. We weren't happy about it, but it's not the end of the world, especially since he's not even wrestling in today's tournament. And speaking of today's tournament. We are in Rocky Hill for the Doc Myers Wrestling Tournament, where my old buddy Paul Myers is the head wrestling coach. Many years ago, I wrestled with his younger brother John Myers in the Junior Olympics, who now coaches a powerhouse nationally ranked team in Poway, California.

Today's tournament is extra special to me for a lot of reasons. One, Paul Myers and I go way back on the coaching circuit. Also, Paul's dad, the former Dr. Edward Myers, was my high school gym teacher in East Hartford, where he was a legend. Dr. Myers refereed the 1964 and 1968 Olympic Wrestling Trials. He was also the football coach, wrestling coach, and athletic director, and gym teacher at my old high school. I think he even started our wrestling program... I'm also thinking about writing a book about East Hartford Wrestling someday, which would obviously include Dr. Myers in it. So, talking with his son Paul today was extra special today.

We got off to a rough start today with our first two guys losing. Coach Torres pulled the whole team into the locker room and just ripped into them about how they're not being real men. Real men suck it up and find ways to fight to the bitter end. Real men don't give up and let themselves be pinned. Coach was furious! However, after everyone left the locker room to go back to the gym, I called the two wrestlers who had just lost back in. Then I went over what they could have done differently to win those matches. And hopefully, next time, they will win their matches.

Our sick team struggled through the day, and Dakota looked really bored up in the stands. We did have some bright spots, though. Our 138- pound senior captain lost a thriller in the semi-finals by just one point. Then wrestled back and convincingly took third place. Our sophomore 160-pounder took first place while sick. Our 182-pounder, also ill, dropped down to the 170-pound weight class and had an absolutely thrilling day of wrestling. He's our warrior. And we never know which way his matches will go.

In the semi-finals, the score was 9-9 with nine seconds on the clock. Our boy went into attack mode and threw the other boy to his back for a huge win that put the whole gym on its feet. In the finals, with about 20 seconds left on the clock and down by one point, he went on attack mode again. He lifted his kid up off the mat for what looked like another amazing win. Only this time, it was thwarted on the way down by his opponent, causing him to lose the match and take second place as time expired and everyone in the gymnasium came to their feet once again. Both boys deserved the tremendous applause they both got.

On another note, our 170-pounder also did an exhibition match against Rocky Hill's autistic wrestler. Our standout wrestler gracefully let the boy take him down. He then let the other boy throw a half-nelson on him. Coach Rogers went through the motions and yelled, "Look away." Our boy put on a pretend struggle and then let the autistic wrestler turn him to his back. The referee slapped the mat while blowing the whistle. The boys got back to their feet, shook hands, and the referee raised the hand of the Rocky Hill boy in victory. The crowd went wild once again for a match and performance that our 170-pounder made possible. It was one of those great moments in sports. And both boys deserved the overwhelming applause that they got. Coach Rogers and I melted when we saw the smile on the Rocky Hill boy's face when he came over after the match to shake our hands…

Another good week of wrestling… A tough one for sure… but another good one!

Here's a poem I found at the Doc Myers Tournament that I want to share with you.

THE WINNER

The winner of a match is a matter of opinion.
This is sometimes lost in a victory's celebration.
The winner is not the one whose hand is raised,
It's not the person a sportswriter praised.
No matter how bad a wrestler is beat,
With his head hanging low,
Walking back to his seat,
The winner is the one who bites his lip and tells himself
It'll be different next trip.

The winner is not one to lay back on a win,
He will not stop until he gets the pin.
He can be behind by 14 points,
He may be aching in muscles and joints,
But you can be sure, no matter how much time remains,
He'll be hustling all the time and forget his pains.

If you say to yourself, I tried my best,
Then you know, win or lose, you're as good as the rest.

Sure it's nice to get 1 place at States,
And be recognized as one of the all-time greats.
But a time will come when someone will say,
I remember him, he was a scrapper in his day.
The winner is not always the champion of the contest.
It's the person who works hard and never rests.
The word "Winner" has lost its meaning.
And the scores in the paper can often be deceiving.
To please the crowd is always a lot of fun,
But only you can get satisfaction from a job well done.
It's not always easy to meet the demands
of those that are yelling for you up in the stands.
The winner is the one who can take a defeat,
His good sportsmanship tells that only in the score was he beat.
He'll always be the winner, in this he can take pride,
If deep in his heart he knows that he tried.

By Steve Greenly

Brian Preece: I have to give Dakota a lot of credit for going to practice after practice and meet after meet despite not having the chance to compete. This is truly remarkable even though he might not think it is a big deal. It is truly rare. I know Dad Daniel being a coach has a lot to do with him being there but even still, Dakota is a free

111

agent and could tell Dad and his coaches, I'd rather be doing something else with someone else. I have to give Dakota further credit for his attempts to make his needed weight despite being a few pounds overweight naturally and not being able to wrestle and do other things that would help his cause. I think this takes both a lot of discipline and motivation.

As a coach, I had plenty of injured wrestlers and even wrestlers that were injured over a long period of time. But I can't think of any in the latter that showed the dedication Dakota has. Even if they came back to compete, they missed a few practices here or there (as in not coming at all). And, as a coach, I can't say I got all that worked up about it maybe like I could or should have. But sometimes as a coach you are more worried about the wrestlers that are working out with the team. I think that's natural. But I hope Coach Torres, and other members of the coaching staff, are noticing the dedication of Dakota. Because what he is doing is truly unusual, even for the coach's kid. It is understandable that he might be a bit bored in the stands at a wrestling tournament. They are pretty long.

And about being bored at wrestling events, this is something the wrestling community needs to work on a bit. And USAWrestlingUtah has done a lot of good things in this area working with the high school coaches hosting different youth events. I wonder if Connecticut and other states are doing this but our youth tournaments now have staggered starts and some get done in as little time as an hour. The idea is to set up your mats, and use Track Wrestling of course, and bring in an entire age group and wrestle them until they're done and then bring in the next age group and wrestle them until they're done and so forth. Some of the larger age groups might take up to a couple of hours or so, but the idea is that parents can bring their children and get in and out at a reasonable time. If you're a seventh-grader, you might be wrestling at 1:00 p.m., but the pre-K group might be right at 9:00 a.m. That's the general trend, start the younger kids sooner. And except for the biggest and more prestigious tournaments, a typical weekend tournament hosted by a high school to raise some money will put wrestlers into groups of four usually and give the competitors three matches.

This is so way better than when I was a youth wrestler where things started early and ended sometimes close to midnight. There were no thoughts of limiting the size of weight classes, staggering starts, or assigning weight classes and age groups to mats for the entire day. The non-stop microphone use was also mentally draining, but sometimes with tournaments now, you can go for hours, or at least a nice chunk of time without having the microphone being used. All of this has made youth wrestling, and high school wrestling, a lot better. And though high school tournaments are structured a bit differently, some similar principles can be used. But there are a lot of things that need to be done by coaches and other leaders in the wrestling community to make wrestling events more fan-friendly, parent-friendly, and competitor-friendly.

I bring up Track Wrestling here and there because I think Justin Tritz, who started it, is one of the most important pioneers in modern wrestling. And he brought together his two loves of computer programming and wrestling and revolutionized a sport. You could say I was one of the early adopters in our state and country for that matter, and when the NCAA finally used Track Wrestling for its matside scoring at its championships, I got the invite with my buddy Andy Unsicker and his son Chad to score.

It was a lot of fun but a bit nerve-wracking. I mean, who wants the Brands' brothers in your face if you screw up something on the score clock, or even if you didn't and they think you did? But it was very cool to meet Tritz, and I think I gave him a suggestion that he incorporated in his scoring program. He invites and even uses suggestions because with any computer program it has to be user-friendly, and it has been incredible to see the changes in Track Wrestling itself since it was adopted about 15 years ago.

My Dad was an early adopter of using technology in the wrestling meets but of course early computer programs for tournaments had their issues. But he really loved technology. He wasn't an old school coach in that regard, in fact, he always had a visionary mind. In the late 1990's he was using computerized maps for traveling way before Google maps came about, and loved what it could do for one of his other hobbies or passions-genealogy. He died before Track Wrestling was developed but he would have loved it and would have marveled that he could track his wrestlers by use of a cell phone, that you could follow a tournament anywhere with the Internet, or now through a computer or TV screen, watch a high school wrestling tournament that uses Trackcast. FloWrestling is great as well and I think the two have, and are, revolutionizing wrestling.

But even as I say this, we as (high school) coaches can do a lot more to promote our sport and make it more fan-friendly. I would say for starters, at your dual meet, just have a program, something tangible to hand out to fans that show who is wrestling who. My programs went a bit further as I talked about possible match-ups to watch, and there was a lot there for our fans like highlights of prior meets, "Wrestlers of the Meet", the upcoming schedule, among other things. Maybe with Track Wrestling, everyone can just pull out their phone or whatever, but I think there's just something to having something tangible in the hands, something you could put in your scrapbook, or just something easy to just glance at. I learned this from my father, who way back in the 1960's and 1970's had hard-stock programs for the fans.

CHAPTER NINE

THE BALANCING ACT OF

COACHING AND FAMILY

Dan Blanchard: I had to record a couple of episodes for my weekly Mindalia TV show tonight, so I missed practice. I'm not liking this missing a practice thing much, but it is what it is, I guess. Sometimes as an adult, duty calls.

When I first talked about possibly becoming one of the coaches of my son's high school wrestling team, most people shook their heads in disbelief. They said that there was no way I would also fit coaching into my already dizzying schedule. I told them that I couldn't just give up everything I do beyond my daily 7 a.m. to 3 p.m. teaching job. But coaching my son and his team for the short amount of time that he will be in high school is important enough for me to scale back, tighten my belt, and find a way somehow to do it.

I believed that anytime with me on the mat is better for Dakota and his teammates than no time with me. And I can't let working a myriad of jobs and life's stressors keep me from this opportunity to be of service. My son, his team, their school, and the development of our community's young men is something I can help out with. I figured if I could find a way to be there on that wrestling mat with those boys trying to find their way to manhood, then that would be a massive victory for all of us.

However, it would not be fair for me to accept a paid job and not be there all the time. That dilemma worked itself out, though, because I am now a volunteer coach. I don't get paid a single penny to be the assistant wrestling coach for my son's high school team. This is an arrangement that I consider to be a win-win, and I'm pleased about it. It's about twenty-five hours a week with my son and his teammates.

I know I have a lot to offer my son and his teammates. And our local high school personnel have gone the extra mile to put the wrestling team and me together on favorable terms to both parties. I guess this is one of those cases of creative problem-solving. It's incredible what we can figure out when we work together instead of against each other.

After wrapping up the recording of two television shows, I jumped in my car and drove over to the high school. My son, Dakota, was exiting the building right as I was pulling up. On the way home, we had the liveliest talk that we've had in a while. Today was Dakota's first day of being back on the mat drilling wrestling moves with the other wrestlers and doing some conditioning. No LIVE wrestling, though...

On the way home, Dakota gave me the play-by-play on how practice went. He was excited, and I could even see that he was happy to be tired and worn out again. Dang... I wish I was there... My wife wished I was there, too... She was a little worried about how Dakota's knee would handle his first day of drilling. She wanted me there to pull him out if I saw that it wasn't going well.

But tonight, we had to rely on Coach Torres and Rogers to make that call of whether or not Dakota's knee was holding up. And it appears that it all went well... Maybe Dakota's comeback really will happen... From this first practice back drilling, it sounds like it will, even if he did get a black and blue above his knee tonight. Not to worry about it, though. It wasn't on his knee but above it.

When we got home, Dakota even told me, without me asking, that he worked on his stance tonight to more closely mimic the stance I used to use when I was in high school. I've been talking to him for over a year now on his stance. But he wanted to do things his way. I'm pumped that he is finally seeing the logic in improving his stance.

Dang...! I wish I was there tonight. I wish I didn't have to miss this awesome comeback practice that Dakota just had. And I wish that I didn't have to miss tomorrow night's practice, too. Adult duty calls again... I have my elected union officer job to attend to tomorrow night. This will draw me away for the second night in a row from wrestling practice... Hopefully, Dakota's practice goes just as well as tonight's did...

Tuesday was a long day. After teaching all day, I went to my local union job in New Britain for a couple of hours. I then went to my state-wide union position in Rocky Hill for a couple of more hours. By the time I got home, I was exhausted and not quite ready for the robust greeting I walked into the moment I came through my front door.

Dakota's knee was causing him pain again. And the coaches were asking him to go to the doctor's to get permission to wrestle all three matches this upcoming Saturday. My wife, Dakota's mom, wasn't having any of that. And she let me know it. She was frustrated. Dakota was frustrated. And now I was really frustrated… I'm just not sure how this is going to turn out… And I can see that it's eating at my boy…

Today, we will wrestle the tough Bristol Central at home. Dakota checked his weight this morning, and he was two pounds over. Since his knee was hurting last night, I'm not sure that he can make weight today. Nor if he should even try since he's probably shouldn't run on it. And he's not wrestling tonight anyway.

Later in the day, a text from my wife frustrated all of us, even more, when she shared that Dakota is having sharp knee pains in school… Shortly after that, Dakota sent a picture via text that shows his knee is all swollen up again… Dang… This is driving me crazy… Maybe I should just sit him for the next two months…

As expected, Bristol Central brought a skilled, very large, and powerful team to our gymnasium tonight. Unexpectedly, Dakota made weight, even though he couldn't run. He won't be wrestling tonight. To his mother's dismay, he spits off eight-tenths of a pound after not eating all day.

Well, things went well for Bristol Central, but not so well for us. We lost the first several matches right out of the gate and didn't manage to get on the board until our 138-pound senior captain stepped onto the mat at the 145-pound weight class. He wrestled a tough kid who put him on his back once. But our captain was able to fight his way through it and win the match anyway. After the meet, I showed him a couple of things he could have done differently.

Our next win came from our 160-pound sophomore and then another from our 170-pound junior who used to be our 182-pounder. Both of these boys wrestled very tough and beat pretty good kids.

And that was it for our wins tonight—just three. But, what might have been even worse was seeing our 132-pound sophomore still sitting on the bench with a large knee again. Everyone wants Dakota to wrestle again, but his knee just won't cooperate. And even though I love wrestling, in my view, the health of his knee is what's really important here.

Also, I believe that wrestling is the tool or vehicle one uses to build a good man. But in the end, it's just the tool or vehicle. Wrestling is not the end goal or destination in my mind. Becoming a good man of character is the end goal or destination through the use of wrestling if it's available. And if it's not available, and one has to use a different tool or vehicle for a while to head toward that destination of becoming a good man, then we go to plan "B." Remember, there are many roads to Rome and many ways to become a good man.

But, in the meantime, we will continue to take this day by day and see what happens. Maybe Dakota can make it back for the States, and perhaps he won't.

On Thursday, Dakota's knee is still swollen. Ironically, even though Dakota didn't have a doctor's appointment, the doctor's note of release allowing him to wrestle again came today. But the school trainer said Dakota wasn't ready to wrestle today after looking at his knee. Dakota spent the practice riding the bike again. The coaching staff and Dakota were frustrated beyond belief.

Friday, Dakota had physical therapy. And my wife had a long talk with the physical therapist. He is being cautious but believes there is still a chance that Dakota can somehow make it back for States if everything goes perfectly. Dakota doesn't mind having to ice a swollen knee every night. But, for today's practice, Dakota is not to wrestle. He is only to do physical therapy stuff.

I approach Head Coach Torres with a plan to get Dakota back for the States. Coach doesn't like it and says he's going to pull Dakota for the rest of the season. I talked him out of it and convinced him to continue to take it day-by-day and wait and see. When practice finished, Coach Torres approached me again and said that he thought about it some more and that he would sit Dakota for the rest of the season… He just can't see sense in putting Dakota through the grueling strain of a State Tournament without the necessary practices to be ready for it. This was a hard pill for me to swallow. And I couldn't say anything at the time. All I could do was sigh.

Saturday was a great tournament in Colchester, even though Dakota didn't wrestle in it. He was happy, though, that he didn't have to make weight for this one. I followed the bus up because I had to leave mid-day to bring my two youngest girls to their futsal games while my wife helped out our two oldest daughters. The first two rounds went well for our boys. Just last night, they were looking like George Washington's ragtag army, where they all appeared either sick or hurt. But, like real warriors, they sucked it up when the duty of wrestling called them into combat for each match.

Very early in the day, I ran into my old East Hartford wrestling buddy, Ryan Fitch, the head coach of RHAM. He had somehow found out that Dakota's knee had swelled up again. He said he was sorry and that I should probably sit him for the rest of the season.

Later, while consoling one of our kids who had just been pinned. I tried to explain to him that what really matters is that he is making the commitment to getting better and tougher every week, and not this loss. As I was talking to him, someone overhooked me from my blindside. I turned and saw my old East Hartford buddy Pat Moynihan whose two boys wrestle for the powerhouse wrestling team Xavier. Immediately I feigned a hip-toss on him followed up by the chain wrestling of a back-trip. It was so cool to see my buddy that goes all the way back to the second grade. After a short talk about our sons, he agreed that I should sit Dakota for the rest of the season.

Late morning I took off and got my girls over to their futsal (Brazilian soccer) games. They both played well and had fun. We won our first game and lost our second. Even though we lost our second to a team that we already beat, I believe, according to the point system, we're still in first place in the league.

The girls and I drove to Dakota's wrestling tournament just in time to see the medal rounds. My little girls kept pulling at my shirt to go play tag with them. I kept telling them we had a wrestler coming up, so we had to wait. And since we had five boys in the medal rounds, they had to wait quite a bit. But at the same time, we also managed to pull off a few short rounds of playing tag too away from the wrestling.

While I was waiting for our boys to wrestle, I ran into another one of my old East Hartford wrestling buddies, Kevin Kanaitis. Kevin is the former Head Coach of RHAM and a wrestling referee. His parents were there too. And I couldn't help but reminisce for a moment how his parents were also there 35-years ago watching me and Kevin's older brother, Scott, wrestle. Now they were there again watching their grandchildren while we watched our children wrestle. You gotta love the wrestling community. It's a tight-knit clan. And even when people do drift away, they often find themselves years later, drifting right back into it again.

Well, our 138-pound senior captain did it again with another first-place victory. Our 170-pound junior finished second. Our 160-pound sophomore finished 3rd. And our 113-pound sophomore finished 5th, as well as did our 126-pound junior. It was a pretty good day for a team that was looking so beat up yesterday at practice. However, I can't help but wonder how Dakota would have done today...

Brian Preece: As I read Daniel's story for this week, my first thought went to my decision to coach and its impact on my family. Coaching wrestling means time away from my family. My son Zach didn't wrestle, never had an interest, and I declined to force him, guilt him, or even influence him in any shape or form. Athletics aren't his thing. But being a great person is his thing. Zach is a person who serves others and does his best in school. He got involved in some service clubs. He also ran some cross-country and did some track and that was good enough for me.

His older sister Lizzy was not much interested in athletics either. She is an amazing student and did some dance, choir, and orchestra in her school years. And she became a manager at age 17 at one of the busiest restaurants in our state.

Both of my children have great work habits. But they weren't too interested in wrestling. I retired from being a head coach in 2006 when my daughter was just six and my son was four. But I have remained very involved in the sport running events, officiating, announcing, and writing. I did, however, take on a smaller role as an assistant wrestling coach for three years while in "retirement". I also continued coaching golf and football here and there, as well as a lot of baseball, a sport I truly love. And in Utah, if you teach core Social Studies classes, you can expect to teach 200 plus students. (I don't exaggerate, I taught over 200 students in all but two years of my 30 years teaching and for two years I taught nearly 285 students.)

I had so many great experiences teaching and coaching, but sometimes I wish I had spent more time with my own children versus other people's children. I wish I would have ingrained my own family into my coaching experiences a bit better. I have seen some coaches successfully do that. However, I remember always being tired. So, when the odd weekend rolled around where I didn't have a wrestling tournament or a baseball practice, sometimes I wasn't as emotionally available to my family as I could have been. My wife Heidi often joked about my need to be in my "cave". And while I felt I needed my "cave time", I know this came at a cost, which sadly was less meaningful experiences with my wife and children.

Before the days of laptop computers, I also remember going to my high school to work on Sundays to grade papers, input grades and do lesson plans. Many times, my assistant coach Darren Hirsche was already there doing the same. During some of those years, he taught even more students than I did if you can believe that. We typically did this after coaching Friday and Saturday at some weekend invitational. And now on our one supposed "day off" we were back at school, exhausted, and frantically trying to catch up and plan for the next week of teaching our classes. We had to stay on top of our main job as classroom teachers. Quite honestly, my teaching ability paled compared to Darren's. But that's what teacher-coaches do and Daniel certainly knows my life and the sacrifices that come with it.

I know I made an internal decision not to force my kids into sports, or really anything extracurricular. I have always felt conflicted because of my own experience with my parents, and my Dad specifically, about how I should handle this with my own children. As a youngster, I was often forced to go to a lot of sporting events unwillingly. Without my consent, my parents signed up for things like soccer. And nothing against soccer, but I had no interest or ability whatsoever in the game. My sister played soccer well, and my brother was pretty good at it. But he eventually decided it conflicted too much with baseball.

As I alluded to in mine and Dan's first wrestling book, *Hitting the Mat*, I had to have some frank discussions with my Dad about wrestling, and to his credit, he listened. Though, I know it was hard for him to hear the message. I said I would wrestle for my school teams, but I had no interest in doing much in the "off-season". So I gave up doing freestyle in the ninth grade. And I actually started to enjoy wrestling again, and I think my relationship improved with my parents, too. But I think it was hard for my Dad to hear that I didn't want to wrestle that much because I'd rather golf, ski, or work. What I wanted meant less time for us to be together in his wrestling world.

Being in my mid-fifties and retired, caused me to look back and take stock of my life. What's next? Well, a big part of that is spending more time with my wife Heidi. I try to do more things to make her life easier and try to spend more time with my adult children. I know there is no make-up for time lost, but I am trying to be forward-thinking. My daughter is married, so I'm no longer the most important man in her life. But her husband, Jacob, is a good dude. And I'm grateful that my son likes to go on long drives in the countryside where we can talk about life, and listen to some good music from past to present.

I know this season has been tough for Dakota. He hasn't been able to get on the mat to compete. And of course, it has been frustrating for Daniel, his Dad, and the coach. But hopefully, even if the season wasn't ideal, both will cherish their time together. And wrestling has provided that vehicle for that to happen for them.

CHAPTER TEN

IT'S GREAT WHEN YOUNG PEOPLE EXCEED OUR EXPECTATIONS!

Dan Blanchard: Well, it's getting into the second week of February, and wrestling season is winding down. Monday and Tuesday's practices were pretty typical. The wrestlers did a bunch of spinning, some drilling, some stretching, and then some live wrestling. Then they did some more spinning followed by sprints to finish off the practice. Dakota was also once again back up on the bike doing his own kind of spinning.

Tuesday night, Dakota and I talked about off-season wrestling when the practice was over. I told him that he had three or four weeks to do his physical therapy exercises religiously. Dakota needed to get his knee ready for the off-season, or he'll miss that too. He can't afford to miss the off-season if he wants to be a state champ before he graduates in just two short years from now. Hopefully, he'll be ready to wrestle this spring, and it will at least somewhat make up for this missed sophomore season of wrestling.

While talking about off-season wrestling, Dakota and I had an enthusiastic conversation about wrestling again on the car ride home. It was like the ones we used to have last year and at the beginning of this year when his hopes were still high on having a great sophomore year. Sadly, lately, the car rides home have been low-key. We haven't had a ton to talk about this season since he hasn't been wrestling. But now that we're looking at the off-season wrestling again, we had a great conversation. Dakota seemed invigorated like there was hope again. It seems like there is a chance of light at the end of the tunnel through Plan B.

Hopefully, Dakota can get his knee healthy over the next several weeks. We're crossing our fingers. And now we're determined to get ready for tomorrow night's home match against Windsor High School. It's our last home match of the season and our big Senior Night.

Wednesday night is here, and Senior Night was pretty cool. Our female wrestling managers decorated the gym. Some extra wrestling fans showed up to honor our lone senior wrestler, our 138-pound captain, Quin. Quin is Coach Rogers' son. Coach and his wife, Valerie, escorted Quin to the wrestling mat center where Coach Torres and I were waiting to greet them. I shook Quin's hand, then Coach Rogers', and then handed Valerie flowers accompanied with a hug. Coach Torres did the same and told Quin that he really is going to miss him after he graduates and how he better come back to visit.

After a long applause, Valerie broke off toward the head table. She grabbed the microphone to sing our country's National Anthem. She sang beautifully, and then the wrestling meet began. It was a great night of wrestling. Coach Torres bumped Quin up to the 145-pound class, where Quin pinned his opponent and helped us win the meet by one point. When the Windsor boy came over after to shake our coaches' hands, he told Coach Rogers that his son is a BEAST!

It was a pretty exciting night, and everyone seemed to be in good spirits, even Dakota, who once again could only watch from the team bench. Later on, I found out that Dakota had some candy in his pocket and that he had been discreetly snacking on it all night. I guess he's taking advantage of not having to make weight for a while. But, that will be short-lived if we can get his knee back in shape for off-season wrestling.

Dakota and his mom saw his doctor again on Thursday. His doctor told Dakota that the knee is coming along well and that the puffiness is not unexpected. When he was doing the drilling, even though it was light, his knee was yelling out, "What the heck is this? I'm not used to this", which caused fluid to run to his knee, which caused it to swell and hurt again. And when he bends his knee, he's to picture a balloon being squeezed. Just like a balloon being squeezed, when Dakota bends his knee, he is pushing some of the fluid out of the front of his knee. This forces the fluid to the sides and back of his knee. Now, the extra fluid there is what is causing him to be unable to bend his knee all the way.

The good news is that the doctor didn't seem overly concerned. He told Dakota to keep riding the bike but go even harder to build up the muscles in his thighs and around his knee. And then to put on his compression sleeve and ice it every night. Eventually, the swelling will go back down, and the knee should be okay. Let's keep praying, though, anyway… just in case…

After Dakota filled me in on his doctor visit, I gave him a hug good night. As a budding wrestler, he couldn't help himself; he gained inside control and gave me a big bear hug. I playfully backed out my hips some as a wrestler does, and then Dakota really started squeezing. That's when I heard a funny noise come from my rib and felt a shooting pain. I urged Dakota with a bunch of quick pats on his back to let go, but it was already too late. The damage had been done. I'm sure I have at least a bruised rib that is aching every time I cough now. I wonder how many days I'm going to have to live with this discomfort. And I'm also wondering why the heck my rib bruised so easily. Well, I guess at 50-years old, I'm not used to wrestlers squeezing the life out of my ribs anymore, so maybe that's why it damaged so easily.

Friday morning, Valentine's Day, I woke up feeling terrible. I now have a full-blown cold. It's causing me to cough non-stop, and my rib is jumping out in pain with each cough. The ironic thing is that Dakota was at the doctor's yesterday, and he is going to physical therapy today. Now I feel like maybe I should be going to the doctor and physical therapist right alongside Dakota.

I emailed the great Dan Gable today to ask him a question about wrestlers and sickness. When I was a wrestler and a young coach, we didn't want our wrestlers in the wrestling room if they were sick because they'd get other wrestlers sick. And trying to wrestle while sick is a total nightmare. However, some of today's coaches feel that the wrestlers can sweat the germs out of their bodies, so they should be at practice and wrestling with their teammates.

Dan Gable was more in tune with my philosophy of not getting your teammates sick. If you really want to be there and do some sweating, ride the bike, but don't do physical contact with the other wrestlers. I remember how I used to take the day off from physical activity when I was sick and just sit in the steam room to sweat some of it out of me. Then I'd go home to bed.

Well, today, as a coach, I'm sick like several of our wrestlers are too on this Friday. So, I will be coaching from afar today from off the side of the wrestling mat. Nobody needs my germs. Luckily, Dakota's health is good. He shows no signs of this nasty cold that is going through our team. Friday's practice was good but very difficult for our boys, who were slightly under the weather.

Saturday, we had a great day at the CCC Divisional Tournament over at Bristol Central High School. Fourteen teams showed up, and we had a long, good day of wrestling. Our 138-pound senior captain took first. And so did our 170-pound junior. They are both now CCC Champs. Our 126-pound junior took 4th, and so did our 160-pound sophomore. Finally, our 113-pound sophomore took 5th. It was a good showing in a big challenging tournament. Once again, I can't help but wonder how Dakota would have done. Oh, well, I guess we'll have to wait until next year to find out.

While at the tournament, I ran into one of my old Junior Olympic teammates from back in the mid-80s. I was walking past mat one when someone up in the stands yelled my name. I looked up and saw the nearly 50-year old version of my old buddy and teammate, Andy Torres. We had a great talk catching up. And when I asked him who he was here to see, he just smiled and said that he needed a little dose of wrestling today, so he came to watch on a whim. I smiled and told him that my old buddy Tom Berry had said something similar a few weeks ago when I bumped into him. Boy, there really is something about wrestling…

Now… let's see what next week brings. It should be an exciting one. For most of our wrestlers, the season will end this weekend at the Class "L" State Tournament right back at Bristol Central High School. Only time will tell how this is all going to unfold. Who will step up? Who will not? Who will be sick or hurt? And who will beat the odds and amaze us all?

Brian Preece: Daniel got me thinking about the 1993-94 wrestling team at West High School where I was an assistant coach. It was a magical season that year. We won some tournaments including our region (league) tournament, were undefeated in dual meets, and placed second as a team at the tournament my Dad started long ago in Vernal- the Uintah Tournament of Champions. With that all said, we still weren't the favorites to win the state title, it would be the Pleasant Grove Vikings.

Pleasant Grove was the main rival to Uintah when my Dad coached there. Darold Henry was the architect of the extremely successful Pleasant Grove program but had since turned the reins over to one of his former state champion wrestlers, Tom Phelon. But the Viking program at this point wasn't missing a beat. As I have mentioned before, in Utah, teams can qualify two wrestlers per weight class to the state tournament. I think both Pleasant Grove and West qualified around 18 wrestlers that year. Also, in Utah at that time, the state tournament was held over three days. The first two rounds were held the first day, the semifinals and two consolation rounds on the second day, and the placing rounds (the top six) on the final day.

After day one, we were holding our own against the Vikings. However, the semifinal round didn't go quite as we had hoped. We put four into the championship finals but Pleasant Grove put through an incredible amount of nine wrestlers in 14 weight classes. And in regards to the race for the gold trophy, it was game over. Not only were we too far behind Pleasant Grove, but we also found ourselves in third place behind Payson, a team coached by my former BYU teammate, Chris Brown.

I won't say that I was even close to Brown's league as a wrestler. I was a scrub compared to him. He was a Western Athletic Conference (WAC) champion. He was about two or three years ahead of me in school and was named the head coach of Payson while I was still in college. Brown was a good coach, especially with the technique. Payson made huge strides finishing second in the state a couple of seasons in the early 1990s. They were also in the same region as Pleasant Grove, which was the best league in the state for wrestling.

Our region didn't provide much of a challenge and I was always a bit worried about that. Eventually, I was able to convince our head coach, Don Holtry, to attend stronger tournaments like the Tournament of Champions. But in our region dual meets, we were still hardly ever challenged. And I am of the mindset that tougher competition, even if it means a few more losses for our team and individual wrestlers, was a better formula generally for success.

After the semifinal round, Payson had put six wrestlers into the championship finals and was about 10 to 15 points ahead of us. We still had one advantage, we had six guys still alive (or not beat out) of the tournament fighting back for third place in the consolation matches, while Payson just had three.

I know I had a sleepless night. In fact, I know I was up until around three o'clock in the morning studying brackets, going through the possible scenarios, and so forth. I know it might sound counterintuitive to hard-core sports enthusiasts, but I really wanted to get that second-place trophy. Our athletic association gives out trophies to the top two teams and I just wanted one for our school and for our head coach, Don Holtry. At that time, Don was in his 24th year as the head coach and had some good runs over the years with a few teams finishing third or fourth. And there were at least one or two years where some incredibly bad luck kept West from finishing in the top two. So I just wanted a trophy for him mostly.

I finally dozed off and got maybe two hours of sleep before my alarm woke me up. I was as nervous as a cat on a hot tin roof to use a movie metaphor. But what happened next was truly one of the most special memories I have in coaching. Our boys came through and then some. They truly exceeded my expectations. We had four guys come back and finish third, each with their own remarkable story. Two were upset in the semifinals but got off the deck to deal with personal disappointment to win their next two matches. Another lost a heartbreaker in the quarterfinals and had to win four in a row to take third. And as far as our other third-place wrestler went, we, as coaches, would have been happy if he won a couple of matches in the tournament and maybe got on the podium. Not only did he place third, but he also beat the grappler who beat him in both a league dual and the region championship.

We also had two other wrestlers place, one fourth and one fifth. But what was neat was that these boys didn't just win their matches, they picked up huge bonus points by winning by a pin, technical fall, or major decision, which isn't easy when you are talking about matches against the best wrestlers in the state.

Payson's three wrestlers in consolation took third, fifth, and fifth. So by the time the championship matches arrived, we had gone out in front. They still outnumbered us in the championship finals six wrestlers to four, so things were still a bit up for grabs. We won two of our four championship finals and they went 1-5. So, when the dust finally settled we had beat them by 22.5 points for second place.

I should also mention the remarkable story of our 119-pound wrestler, Chad Huffman. He upset a Payson wrestler in the quarterfinals, which ended up being huge in the final team tally. He then won his next match in the semifinals, but toward the end of the second round of that bout, Chad started holding his arm and he was noticeably in discomfort. He was up by a lot of points so he was able to get through his match giving up only a few points in the last round to still win.

In the championship finals, he had his arm wrapped up. I'm not sure Coach Holtry knew, and certainly none of us assistant coaches did, but he had broken his arm in the semifinals. Chad had a very severe break in that arm a few years back and had a plate and screws placed in his arm. That's where the new break was at. He lost his state championship match, 7-3. He was taken down right off the bat, thrown on his back in a cradle but valiantly fought off his back and wrestled really well the rest of the match, though falling short in the end. I mean a 5-0 lead is a pretty big one to overcome against a high-caliber wrestler, in fact, a wrestler that would end up being a 4X state champion.

Chad now owns a restaurant in Keystone, Colorado, just on the west side of the Loveland pass at around 8,000 feet in elevation. And when I find myself in the Front Range area of Colorado, I try to make it over to his place, the Haywood Cafe. One of the neatest experiences in my life was taking my two best friends Darren Hirsche, who coached with me for over a decade, and Erik Holdaway, with whom I have coached youth baseball, to eat at Chad's place. Not only do I recommend the food, as my friend Erik said "it was the best breakfast he ever had," but there aren't too many places this beautiful on planet Earth. The big thing here is that it is so marvelous to see your former athletes happy and doing well. Chad didn't need to take State for me to know he would be a winner in life.

That whole group of boys I really loved. West High School is by far the most diverse school in Utah, not only racially and ethnically, but also economically. We have kids that come from "the Avenues," some of the wealthiest areas in Utah, to some of the rougher neighborhoods you can find in Utah as well, where poverty and gang violence are aplenty. Our team reflected the diversity of our school. And like many teams, brought kids together from divergent backgrounds.

Our coaching staff was also pretty diverse. Our head coach was not just the head wrestling coach but the head football coach and a prominent religious leader in the Church of Jesus Christ of Latter-day Saints (also known as the Mormon Church). I guess I was the coaching nerd who scouted the competition and had a notebook of every wrestler our athletes could meet. But I also had strong technique and had brought in my 2-on-1 Step-Thru Turk series to the program. Dan Potts was the longtime assistant of Don and was his first state placer

Don coached. He, like Don, lived in the community for decades. Dan was both a technician and a philosopher and had a very different style of coaching from Don and myself, but it worked with a lot of our boys.

Dan was also great working with our two girl wrestlers, the first ones to take to the mat as high school wrestlers in our state's history. Trust me, Dan was very valuable in helping our program navigate through this new frontier. And Steve Cardon was another very strong technical coach that also came in the room a lot during those years. He wasn't there every day, but he was there enough to bring valuable technique and expertise to our program. And even my future student-teacher Shane Baptista helped out, like Dan, he had a devastating single-leg attack, along with Don's oldest son Greg

We were all a bit different. I have to say that Don was truly a rock. Not just or the wrestling program, but the entire school, the person that most everyone in the community respected, someone they could truly rely on. It was just a magical cohesion of coaching talent that really worked with a very diverse group of kids.

My Dad got involved in the program, too. He did some clinics for us here and there. And he became a huge fan, coming to a lot of our meets. Now my Dad and Don were a bit different in how they coached. I suppose my Dad thought Don was a bit too straight-laced for his liking, but over time, my Dad really started to appreciate Don's coaching talents. Both were men of huge stature, not just physically but as personalities. It was fun to have my Dad take an interest in our program. He even earned the nickname "Papa Preece" from many of our wrestlers. My brother Scott even came in and rolled around with some of our wrestlers, which reminds me of this funny story.

Scott had just returned from serving a two-year proselytizing mission for the Mormon Church in the Philippines. He was pretty thin and fit when he left and he came back even thinner, but not nearly as fit. He wasn't even back a week when he came into wrestling practice. It was time for wrestling and he ended up paired with our Heavyweight wrestler Jeff Holtry, Don's son. Jeff was one of the best wrestlers in our state history. He won three state titles and was an All-American. He won the prestigious Dapper Dan match, the first Utah wrestler to do so.

Though my brother was a state champion himself, it didn't go well against Jeff. My brother hung in there for a few minutes but then he got paler and paler and he was done wrestling for the day after about ten minutes. I'm not sure if he actually threw up, but all of us coaches, and some of our wrestlers, were a bit worried. He insisted he was fine and laid down on some corner of the mat for nearly an hour before we finally managed to get him to his car. My brother was tough and came back the next day. However, this time he worked out a bit more with our other state champion from this team, Brandon Dansie, who wrestled that year at 152 pounds. Brandon ended up taking state twice and was an Academic All-American at the University of Wyoming. He took second in the WAC, and in my view, got hosed out of a wildcard bid to take part in the NCAA tourney, a story for another time I guess.

So as Daniel and his team embark on their state meet next week, I hope that his team would actually exceed his expectations and that a number of his team's wrestlers pull off an upset or two. It's so cool when that happens. That 1993-94 West High team taught me an important lesson. Don't ever sell our young people short!

CHAPTER ELEVEN

DAKOTA'S DEDICATION AND SECOND CHANCES FOR REDEMPTION

Dan Blanchard: Well, this is the last week of the regular wrestling season. This upcoming weekend we will compete in the Class "L" State Tournament. Then the season will be officially over for most of our team. Only a few of our wrestlers will place high enough to extend their wrestling season another week into the State Open Wrestling Tournament for the following weekend.

I'm still sick this week. I cough and sneeze all day long. My rib that Dakota bruised with a bear hug is yelling at me every time I sneeze or cough or hit a bump in the road while driving my car. I also haven't been working out with the wrestlers this week, either. I hate not being hands-on with my instruction. I've been doing my best to coach from afar this week, standing off the side of the mat so I don't get the kids sick. But my throat is sore, and I'm tired and feeling really down. It's kind of bumming me out. Sometimes during practice, I notice Dakota and I are just sitting there off on the side of the mat. We're feeling sort of useless and a bit at a loss at the end of this season.

It's the last week of the season, and it wasn't supposed to end this way for either of us. I wish Dakota, and I were both well enough so we could be LIVE wrestling and getting in great workouts together. And then he could be heading off to the State Tournament with the rest of his team. But, I guess it just wasn't meant to be this year. Maybe next year...

Since I am coaching from afar, I spent some time this week really watching the kids. I studied them some and wondered about them and their stories. What are their past stories that I don't already know about? What will their future stories be?

As I'm scanning the mat, I see that only ten wrestlers lasted until the end of the season. And one of those wrestlers is Dakota, who hasn't wrestled a single day this year. But, he has been at every practice except for that one over Christmas break, where we accidentally locked him out of the building, and he sat outside in the winter weather the entire time.

Our sole female wrestler has also weathered the hardships to get to the end of the season. Very impressive. She will wrestle this weekend in the varsity State Tournament. Wow! She is tough! This is a very tough sport! After all, only ten kids total survived these three months.

It saddens me, though, to think of all the kids that didn't make it to the end as I look around the wrestling mat and see a lot of empty space now where there used to be bodies rolling around in combat. As I continue to scan the mat, I notice something that I haven't seen before. Seven of our ten remaining wrestlers who are leftover are sophomores. Dakota is a sophomore.

If we can keep all of these seven sophomore wrestles, and maybe they can get a few of their friends to come out for the team over the next two years, we could have eight to ten seniors instead of the one that we have this year. Dakota's senior year could produce a fantastic team if everything works out.

We would win a lot of matches with ten seniors on the team. It would be an excellent way for Dakota and his senior class to go out and remember their senior year of high school. Even I didn't have that as a high school wrestler. My best wrestling team at East Hartford High was that 1987 team during my junior year, where I was one of five guys from my team's 'muscle alley' in the Class "LL" State Finals. That was most likely East Hartford's best team ever. My senior year team wasn't as good. We didn't get to go out on top like I had the year before. But, if the stars line up, maybe Dakota's senior year team could be one of their school's best ever… and that would be something to remember for a long time…

As I keep watching Dakota and his team this week while wondering about their stories, my eyes land on a couple of our physically less talented wrestlers. I have coached a lot of these types of kids over the years. They are the ones who aren't rugged. They are the ones that you wouldn't expect to join the wrestling team. However, every year, every team out there has a couple of them battling against all the odds and surviving.

These physically less-talented kids continuously have to wrestle kids who are stronger, faster, and more aggressive than them. They endure and survive these hurricanes that jump all over them and want to beat the heck out of them. Many of these less talented kids refuse to quit and live to fight another day. What they don't have yet as a physical fighter, they more than enough make up for with their mental toughness and psychological stamina. No matter how many times they get taken down, they get right back up and are still part of the now much smaller number of wrestlers still standing there at the end of the season.

It's sort of like the RUDY syndrome from the movie of the boy playing on the Notre Dame Football team. I wish I knew how to tap into these types of kids' magic and share it with all of us... We could all be a little more durable...

My eyes next land on our sole senior wrestler, Quin. He's our 138-pound captain who has been impressive all season long. I wonder where he'll end up after high school. He might join the Marines, which he'll do fine if he goes there because he's a good wrestler. So he'll be able to handle the Marines. He's also an excellent catcher for his high school baseball team. Baseball is his first love, even more so than wrestling. Maybe he'll play baseball in college... Wherever he goes, I know he'll do well because he already has the discipline and knows how to work very hard. I'm sure going to miss him, though, when he's gone. He better come back and visit.

Coach Torres seems a little bit more relaxed this week. He's occasionally joking and rolling around some with the kids. He's jumping in to show them better techniques when he sees one doing something that isn't perfect. However, even though his demeanor is calm this week as if now he knows that he's done all that he can, and now it's their turn to show what they got, he reminds them of something that I will call one of Coach's truisms.

He tells them that he knows some of them are tired and worn out from the long, hard season. He says he knows some of them are sick. He also tells them that he knows some of them are hurt, too. He then tells them that no one will care about any of their problems this weekend in the States. People will only pay attention and care if they win.

It might sound harsh to some of you out there, especially if you're not a wrestler, but it's the cold hard truth in the world of high school wrestling. Did you perform and produce, or not? Coach Torres hit the nail on the head. Win, or go home…

It's been nice having Joey around this year. Joey wrestled on last year's team. That was a pretty good team. Every varsity wrestler, including Dakota, had a winning record. However, we graduated five of the nine kids who wrestled on last year's team, including Joey. Joey is back this year as a volunteer coach like I am. He's so close in age to our wrestlers that he's almost a player-coach, which is good for our team.

However, even though Joey is only a year older than our one senior, Quin, there's still something about him that reminds me how fast these kids grow up. Joey no longer looks like a high schoolboy. In just one short year, he now looks a lot more like a young man. As a coach and educator, I never cease to be amazed by this phenomenon, regardless of how many times I experience it.

Even though Dakota and I are not experiencing the last week of our wrestling season the way we envisioned it. I guess there have been a lot of positives going on all around us. We just take the time to look close enough. For example, I just realized that both Dakota and I have made it through an entire season, and neither one of us caught ringworm. And that's a good thing for both the young wrestler and an old wrestler…

I just thought of another pretty cool thing. After 15 years, I am finally back at a State Wrestling Tournament as a coach. And I don't know if it's just because I'm 15 years older or not, but this weekend tournament felt even longer and harder and more draining than I remember from my first go-around as a younger coach.

There were a lot of ups and downs for our team this weekend. And I saw so many old friends of mine that I lost count. However, something I do remember about my old friends was that their lives have been just as much like a see-saw with ups and downs as ours. Their stories were amazing, and they brought me both joy, sorrow, and sometimes hope while reconnecting with them. The wrestling community is incredible! Come to think of it, I even bumped into several old friends who didn't even have a son wrestling there. They just wanted to come down to watch and be around wrestlers. Pretty cool, huh?

When the dust settled late Saturday night, we had two place winners, a fourth and a second. Earlier during the day, our lone senior captain, Quin, was battling hard in the semi-finals to determine who would go to the finals. Our entire team was on the edge of their seats. We coaches were inching closer and closer toward the center of the mat, leaving our coaching zone that we were supposed to stay in way behind us.

Quin fought like a warrior. But the Simsbury boy was extremely talented with tons of experience and also fought relentlessly. It was a great match. And I really wanted to go out there and help him, especially at the end when the time was running out and Quin was still behind. Time ran out. And Quin would not be in the finals. My heart broke for our senior. He has been dedicated beyond belief to this sport. And now he won't get his dream of being in the finals his senior year. This was his one shot. He doesn't get another chance next year.

I hugged him and told him he did awesome with a lump in my throat and moist eyes. Then I had to take a moment to recompose myself for our next wrestler. There are a lot of ups and downs in wrestling; just ask any wrestler, wrestling coach, or wrestling family. Wrestling is physically and emotionally draining. Quin went on to take fourth, and we're all so proud of him. His weight class was stacked with very talented and very tough wrestlers, which is a tough hand to handle one's senior year.

Our 170-pound junior shocked the crowd a few times this weekend. He pulled off a thrilling victory in the quarter-finals and then came back and did it again in the semi-finals against a very talented Simsbury boy. He made it to the finals on pure grit and determination.

And in the finals, against an overwhelming opponent, he thought he'd go to his bank of grit and determination one more time and perhaps wow the crowd again with his pure courage as our number one brawler.

But, this time, he too came up short. He was distraught that the natural-born fighter in him failed him this time against a technically superior kid. I tried to calm him down by telling him that he had only one job out there. And that job was to go after that other boy with a vengeance. And then let the chips fall where they fall.

Then I told him that he did go after that other boy, but it just didn't work out this time. He spits back that he failed. I told him that he only failed if he didn't go after that kid. And I know that he did. I then tell him that he can't win all of his matches. It just doesn't work that way in life. No one wins all the time, regardless of how hard they try to believe they can.

Brian Preece: Losses at state can be so painful. I remember coming up short myself, the semifinal loss my senior year was the end of my dream of ever becoming a high school state champion, at least as a wrestler. I've been able to coach some state champion wrestlers, but like any coach, most of your wrestlers don't get to the top, their season often ends with a loss.

I did a bit of a shot at redemption for my loss in the semifinals when I wrestled in the All-Star Dual. But it was by sheer accident that this opportunity presented itself.

The All-Star Dual (in Utah back then) took place the Saturday after the state tournament. It was designed to be an exhibition of the state's best wrestlers from the different classifications. At that time Utah had four classifications, now the state has six different classifications. It wasn't as big as what we have now, but regardless, it was still a way to get some of the state's best wrestlers on the mat against each other. For some reason, I decided to go up and watch. It was to be held at Layton High School, about a 45-minute drive from my house in the Salt Lake Valley. I still have no idea why I wanted to go watch this other than sheer boredom. My Dad didn't have any desire to go, so I decided to go alone and watch a couple of friends from other schools who were supposed to be wrestling in the event.

Some top wrestlers turned down the invite. They were tired and wanted the season to be over. But there were still some very exciting matches between multiple state champions and so forth. I arrived just as the line-ups were being introduced. I had my soda and some popcorn and found a spot about halfway up the bleachers. The crowd wasn't huge, mostly parents and other family members.

One of the wrestlers (Steve Geisler) who beat me for third place (in Class 4A, the largest-school classification) was supposed to wrestle the 2A state champion from Delta High School. Delta was a small-school powerhouse in the Beehive State and has won more state titles than any program in our state's history. For a while, they were my Dad's rival at Uintah. My Dad eventually turned the tables in the rivalry in Uintah's favor before reclassification put Delta in 2A and Uintah in 3A for somewhat larger schools. After that, Delta was back to its winning ways. They were very strong in the 1980s, winning nine 2A state titles in a row.

As I was chowing down on my popcorn watching the 119-pound match, Russ Paulsen, the head coach at Bingham High School, and I made eye contact. He was one of the organizers of the event. He waved me to come down to the gym floor.

"Brian, I need a big favor from you," he said. Then he proceeded to tell me how they couldn't find Geisler (and remember this was way before cell phones) and that a bunch of Delta people had driven all the way up to Layton, a trip of around four hours, to watch the event. I reluctantly agreed to take his place. Russ was pretty convincing. We went back to the locker room to a coach's office, and he gave me one of the all-star blue singlets, found me a pair of wrestling shoes, and told me to sit with the "blue" team. He weighed me in and deemed me "close enough". I had no idea what the weight allowance was and at that time I wouldn't have minded being declared overweight. By the time I got dressed, there were just a few minutes to warm up the best I could. I was reminded about the altered rules which combined some aspects of folkstyle and freestyle. The point scoring was the same as folkstyle, but if there was no action on the mat, the wrestlers would return to their feet as they do in freestyle. I wasn't sure I liked the rules because the top position is where I am best. But the bottom was my worst and I figured if I could stall enough, we would go back on our feet, which would be okay.

I guess things were happening so fast I didn't get too nervous about winning or losing. In fact, I was more worried about throwing up my "dinner" of popcorn and a Coke. I hadn't worked out in the last week. I didn't even have any time to stretch properly or drill at all before the match. But as it turned out I was able to win the match 5-4 anyway. I got a couple of takedowns and even got away. And much like my match I had for third place at state, I felt relaxed and just had fun wrestling.

One of my Dad's good friends Paul Dart, the longtime coach at Tooele High School, sat in my corner. After my hand was raised and I went back to the bench, he told me, "your Dad should have been here. That was the best match I have ever seen you wrestle." I was very pleased and proud to show off my All-Star blue singlet to my Dad when I got home and tell him about how I somehow got to wrestle and beat a state champion from Delta.

I think about what Coach Dart said now and then. My father was the greatest coach I knew. However, in most of my best matches, he wasn't present. He wasn't there in this match or when I took fourth in a college tournament. Nor was he there when I won the BYU

Intramurals twice against what I think was some rugged competition. Maybe getting a bit out of his shadow allowed me to relax a bit and better reach my own potential as a wrestler. But it sometimes also makes me sad that he wasn't there for this and other triumphs I had.

Like me, Steve Geisler became a teacher and coach and then went into administration (I didn't do that part). We're friends on Facebook. When I occasionally see him I always say "thanks for not showing up and letting me have the chance to go out a winner." I have asked him what happened, and he told me he didn't even know he was supposed to wrestle. There must have been some communication mishap between the event organizers, his head coach, and so forth. That mishap worked out well for me. It was cool to beat a Delta wrestler, a 2X state finalist, and state champion. It gave me some confidence to consider maybe giving college wrestling a try, which I did for a spell at BYU. Most of all, it took some of the sting out of losing that semifinal match. Losing to Geisler for third and fourth wasn't that big of a deal to me, but losing the night before in the semifinals was the loss that hurt the most in my personal wrestling career.

As a coach, you have many sad conversations in the tunnel. What I mean by the tunnel is that in Utah our state championships are held at a college arena and there is an access tunnel to the arena floor. After the matches are over, that's where the competitors head. And for those who lost, it is where all the emotions of disappointment come out in tears. I have no qualms admitting that I have teared up with my wrestlers. But at the same time, letting them know how proud I am of their successes, their efforts, their hard work, and their willingness to risk. It takes a lot of guts to risk a loss by wrestling in front of thousands of fans. My Dad told me how proud he was of me when I fell short. I remember that conversation and I need my wrestlers to know that I love them and am proud of them.

Many times, as sad as losing in the championship finals or the semifinals is losing in what some people call the "heartbreak round" or the "blood round." In Utah, we place or medal the top six wrestlers. There is a round, where we go from the top eight wrestlers to the top six wrestlers who will all get medals. In Utah, this blood round takes place at the same time as the semifinals. For many wrestlers, placing in State is their big goal, and falling just one match short of that can be devastating, especially for seniors.

I remember my heart went out to one of my senior wrestlers who lost in overtime, 3-1. He was disappointed in the outcome and either pounded the mat in disgust or tossed his headgear, and we were docked a team point.

Back in the tunnel he was in tears and being comforted by his older brother. Then the announcer of the tournament announced that our team was docked a team point just as I was arriving in the tunnel. My wrestler was very apologetic about the team point and letting me down. I know that some coaches would have been upset that their wrestler lost their cool and gave up a team point. But this wrestler was truly a quality young man. He wanted so badly to place in State. He had worked so hard during the season and did just about everything the coaches asked of him. I told him not to worry about the team point and that I was proud of him. The kid that he lost to in overtime had beat him pretty good earlier in the year. This time around, he showed improvement and had wrestled very well. And that's all we could ask of any of our wrestlers.

As Daniel talks about the last matches of his team's top wrestlers, these moments come to mind. But I'm also mindful of Dakota, who didn't get a chance to compete his sophomore season. I take some solace that it's just his sophomore season and hopefully his knee will heal and he will return to action better than ever. But even as I write this, another thing is taking away opportunities for kids to compete all over the country, that scourge that is COVID-19.

In Utah, the pandemic wiped out spring and summer sports for the 2019-20 season. Daniel says it did the same thing in Connecticut. So, they didn't get a chance to test Dakota's knee in any post-season/off-season wrestling. In Utah, we were able to get through some of the fall sports season, though some teams had to sadly forfeit some state tournament football games. In Connecticut, most of the fall sports were canceled.

Now the start of the winter wrestling season has been postponed. And the Wrestling Against Cancer Duals event that I have run for the past ten years to start off the competitive wrestling season, has been canceled. It's been 100 years since we've seen something like this in our country. Let's hope and pray that wrestlers across the country, including Dakota, get a chance to compete in 2020-21. They're all anxiously trying to take that mat.

PART TWO

CHAPTER TWELVE
COVID-19 SHUTS DOWN MOST
OF AMERICA

Dan Blanchard: Wow! November 30th has rolled around again. It's getting to be near the end of the year 2020. This has been one heck of a year for most people around the U.S. and the world.

A lot of things are going on today, as well as not going on today. It's the first Monday after Thanksgiving. And since I was a 14 year-old boy, the first Monday after Thanksgiving always meant that it was also the first day of wrestling season here in Connecticut and my birthday.

Today, I am 51 years-old. For much of my life, November 30th meant wrestling practice as an athlete, coach, and now as a father/coach. November 30th is always a very long day for me. Often my birthday takes a back seat, and we just sort of squeeze it in around everything else that is going on.

However, this year is peculiar because there isn't much going on at all. There is no wrestling happening in Connecticut because of the pandemic. COVID-19 has shut everything down around here, including wrestling. We haven't wrestled here in Connecticut since the last high school season, which ended last February.

My kids were sent home from their schools last March to do remote learning because of the deadly pandemic that was sweeping the globe. And here we are on November 30th, the following school year. All five of my kids are home from school learning remotely, including my college-age daughter, Kalaiya.

So, when I say a lot is going on and not going on... I really mean it. This Coronavirus is crazy and deadly, and it's rapidly spreading more and more each day. But at the same time, my family seldom leaves our home now. We really aren't doing much at all.

I feel really bad for the kids that do extra-curricular activities and really enjoy or even need those extra-curricular activities that have been canceled. For some kids, those extracurriculars are the best part of their day. I'm sure if I asked my boy, Dakota, which one he liked better, he'd probably say he likes the extra-curricular wrestling more than the mandatory school.

Now, that may change someday. But, right now, Dakota is a 16 year-old boy who dreams of winning a state championship in wrestling. Last year, he tried to take the mat, but his knee surgery kept him on the sidelines. Now, COVID-19 eliminated all off-season wrestling and is threatening to destroy this school year's season. Dakota has been dealt an awful hand for someone with the goal to improve every day in wrestling and earn a spot at the top of the awards podium at States.

Like some of the other kids out there, Dakota has a little weight set in the basement. It isn't much, but he's trying to make due. And any kind of workout right now is better than no exercise, right? Dakota has also been running our driveway. We have a very long 465-foot dirt driveway that is slightly uphill all the way. So, with not much else to do, Dakota has been out there trying his best to run it and keep somewhat close to wrestling shape. However, anyone who has ever wrestled before knows that the only way to really stay in wrestling shape is to wrestle.

We really could use a small wrestling mat in the basement. However, we don't have one. Every once in a while, Dakota and I go down to our unfinished basement with its concrete floor and do some slow, deliberate neutral drilling. Again, it's frustrating knowing how limited we are right now. But, again, I guess any kind of workout is better than no workout, right. We're trying to stay positive and do something that will at least help Dakota hold his ground with his skills and conditioning. We can't let this pandemic push him all the way back to square one.

Brian Preece: I feel it would be apropos to comment on the COVID-19 situation here in Utah. It's a bit different than what Daniel and Dakota are experiencing in Connecticut.

Whether it should be or not, COVID-19 has become political. And Connecticut is a liberal state and Utah is one of the more conservative states. While COVID-19 has caused some things to be shut down, or some mask mandates, Utah is far more open in about every aspect than Connecticut. Besides the mask requirement to go into businesses, which many people here in the Beehive State flauntingly ignore, nothing much is shut down. The traffic is much the same as it was pre-COVID-19 giving little indication that a virus is raging in our state or nation. Now Utah did shut down a bit more in the spring, and like Connecticut, spring sports in high school were shut down. My son was a senior and many extracurricular things he enjoyed were also canceled. And he had a unique, but very fun, drive-thru graduation ceremony. But there was some personal disappointment for sure. He was in a club that was going to take a trip to New York City, and that trip was canceled. And for those that did spring sports, it was really sad to see these opportunities taken away.

The Salt Lake School District in the heart of downtown Salt Lake has kept its schools entirely online, but they will go back to in-person classes in January. Meanwhile, the rest of Utah opened up its schools, maybe delaying a week or so, to give teachers some extra time to prepare because even though in-person school was a go, many parents didn't want to send their children back to school so districts have had to make better or more online options available. In Utah, many schools are doing a hybrid model where students go in-person some of the time and do online part of the time with the idea that with fewer students in the building, social distancing would be easier, and there would be less spread to COVID-19. For teachers, this model has been really, really difficult. But because of more demand for online teaching, it has allowed me, as a retired school teacher, to get a side-hustle with my former school district teaching three online courses. And my wife Heidi took a new position in her district where she teaches and gives special education services to online students.

In regards to sports, Utah decided to go full throttle in the fall. I guess Utah high school athletics is much like what they have done in college and pro athletics, if your team has too many COVID-19 cases, your team can be shut down or players aren't allowed to play. But basically, Utah got through fall sports with a few blips. I even coached some high school golf. Sadly, several teams had to forfeit state football playoff games, and there were one or two forfeits in the girl's state soccer tournaments. The saddest story might be where Kearns High School, ranked No. 5 in the state's largest classification, had to forfeit its state football game. Their school district shut them down, then decided to let them play only to pull the plug again one or two days before the game.

But as COVID-19 cases in Utah started to surge in late October and early November, the governor of Utah, Gary Herbert, decided to take more drastic steps including giving Utah a statewide mask mandate. And he also shut down the start of winter sports, including wrestling, for two weeks. Football still had two weeks of the season remaining, but it was decided that it would be the exception, and on the Saturday before Thanksgiving, Utah completed its fall 2020 football season.

However, the start of wrestling season, which is usually the first Monday in November, was pushed back to the Tuesday before Thanksgiving, the date where the first competitions would normally start. Then competition was allowed to start on December 11. But this was a bit sad for me because for the past ten years I've organized and ran an event called "Wrestling Against Cancer." It was an event that brought together about ten schools to do some dual meets to start the competitive season and to raise money for a family battling cancer. But with the late start of the season, it wasn't feasible to do the event.

Our athletic association (UHSAA) has also limited the number of teams, wrestlers, and crowds of wrestling events. This has caused some interesting scheduling quirks. In Utah, the large invitational is quite popular, tournaments with maybe two to three dozen teams. But that isn't allowed with the UHSAA. So some of these schools that do tournaments are doing two tournaments in one as a clever adaptation, doing a tournament on Friday with a set of teams, and then another tournament on Saturday with another set of teams. I think the limit for competitors can be up to 224 if the special exemption is given, otherwise, it is 112 wrestlers.

The UHSAA also sanctioned girl's wrestling this year. However, COVID-19 has greatly reduced the number of wrestlers in our state and maybe has hurt girls wrestling from getting a stronger foundation. A lot of high schools don't have any girls wrestling or a relatively small number. The UHSAA is also deciding how many classifications girls wrestling will have. But as you can see this virus has impacted a lot that is happening in our schools and high school athletics. And some teams are in "quarantine" status as they have too many cases in their programs, and all winter athletes in Utah must be tested weekly.

So while high school wrestling in Utah is up and going, it's a bit weird. Youth wrestling had to shut down until the fall, but it is going on. And an interesting thing has happened. Our youth tournaments have been inundated with wrestlers from surrounding states where everything is shut down. So even though there have been some negative impacts in the number of youth wrestlers in Utah due to COVID-19, it doesn't seem to have impacted youth wrestling events attracting competitors as out-of-state grapplers have picked up the slack.

CHAPTER THIRTEEN

COVID-19: CONNECTICUT VS. UTAH

Dan Blanchard: Well, it's Christmas again, and still no wrestling. Last year at this time, Dakota's sophomore year, he shared with me how badly he just wanted his knee to be fixed up so he could be back on the mat. I shared with him that in this sport you never put off until tomorrow what you can do today. An injury can happen at any time that will sideline you. As a matter of fact, I know he's shooting to be a state champion his senior year. But to be on the safe side, I told him to shoot to do it his junior year just in case an injury or something else unforeseen keep him out of competition during that week of States his senior year.

Now we are in Dakota's junior year, and we had no way of knowing that during this Christmas week, instead of going to practice every day and multiple tournaments, there would be a pandemic that takes wrestling away from us. Even though Dakota's knee is better, we have yet to step on a high school wrestling mat this season. They're telling us that we might start the season on January 19th with no contact or competitions... That doesn't really feel like wrestling to me. Only time will tell what's really going to happen this year in New England... They say the U.S. is approaching 400,000 deaths from this pandemic. That's around the same number we Americans lost during the four years of WWII.

In the meantime, we've been trying to stay positive. I've been working with Dakota a little bit in our basement. But, it's hard to do much down there in our cold unfinished basement with its concrete floor and walls. We mostly work on stance and motion and do some hand-fighting. Dakota's stance has been improving, and so has his hand-fighting. He's not leaving many opportunities open to get inside on him. And he's in way better shape than me, so he wears me out pretty quickly. I wish I was in better shape, so I could do more for him.

However, sometimes I do frustrate him, and he complains that hand-fighting with me is like hand-fighting with a fire hydrant. I take that as a compliment as I remind him that I am the old champ. And even if I'm not in great shape anymore, I still have my good stance, and I can still remember how to hand-fight and be on the inside. These two simple things make it very difficult for my opponents, including Dakota, to have many openings to score on me.

Although my fire hydrant style has frustrated Dakota, it has also forced him into a better stance and better hand-fighting. When he finally does retake the mat, it's going to be hard for his opponents to get inside on him and get good shots. Dakota won't be easy to score upon if he doesn't let the pressure get to him and just does what he knows.

The last two years of Dakota's high school wrestling have put me back in touch with many of my old wrestling friends and acquaintances. It felt like I had come back home to my old wrestling family that I had been away from for so long. However, this COVID-

19 or Coronavirus has taken that away this year. My family and I have been stuck in our home for almost a year now with very little human contact. I miss people, and I miss my old wrestling family that I'm supposed to be hanging out with right now at very long Christmas tournaments. And I know Dakota misses his teammates and all the wrestling friends he has made all over the state, too.

Thankfully, Dakota and I have had one saving grace that has made these very difficult times a tad bit easier. You may remember way back during Dakota's freshman year, some old guy grabbed Dakota at a wrestling practice during the off-season and said, "Long time ago, I wrestled your dad. Now, I wrestle you!" That man was Shirzad Ahmadi. He is an old friend and mentor who I respect dearly. And I am so grateful that he sought out Dakota and worked with him back then.

Well, guess what? Shirzad, who is something like a 23X World Champion, and the only American to ever win the World's in both Greco and Freestyle in the same week, lives practically right down the road. And he has a wrestling room inside of his house. We have a good relationship with Shirzad, and he knows that Dakota and I have been home and not out running around; Dakota does school from home. He allows Dakota to come over every couple of weeks to workout with him. These occasional workouts have been heaven-sent.

Shirzad, who is 70-something, has a very different style than me. I was a super intense wrestler who was very athletic and went 110 miles per hour all the time. Dakota is very athletic, and I taught him some of that intensity, too. Now, Shirzad, a much more relaxed and calculating wrestler, teaches Dakota how to be a patient wrestler and not be in a rush out there on the mat. Shirzad emphasizes stance, hand-fighting, and taking the time to develop an opening for a good shot. He teaches how to be relaxed and only to attack when one has an opening.

It's different than my style, but who am I to argue with a 23X World Champion and a 70+-year-old man who is still wrestling and still winning World Championships. He's the Mr. Miyagi of wrestling. And my son, Dakota Daniel Blanchard, seems to be the new "Danielson" of this era. He's the lone wrestler training with the old master. Maybe I'm romanticizing this a little bit. But it seems like a pretty cool story, doesn't it? The Karate Kid of wrestling... Hey, why not? After all, they do now have that modern-day spin-off of the Karate Kid called "Cobra Kai."

Shirzad's winning ways and longevity are to be envied. Like I already said, his methods are different than mine. He drills more than he LIVE wrestles. I was always the opposite. I just wanted to go into full combat. However, the older and wise me is now coming around to seeing the logic in what Shirzad talks about in not being a bull out there. Rather, emphasizing technique and strategy while avoiding injuries so one can continue to wrestle for many years.

In addition, Shirzad also thinks outside of the present-day wrestling box, as I do. We both feel some of today's coaches are boxing kids in too much on what they allow their wrestlers to do. Many of today's coaches only teach a few moves for wrestlers to master. Shirzad, like myself, believes that a third-year wrestler with only a double leg takedown, going against a 13-year wrestler who has been drilling that double leg a lot longer, will have a hard time scoring.

Shirzad and I both believe that a wrestler needs to be better-rounded and have multiple tricks in his or her bag to go to for scoring.

In addition, Dakota, being a teen boy, has been feeling caged in our home for much of this last year. I have seen him pacing the house looking for something to do. He looks like his teen male testosterone is about to rip out through his skin. The small amount of time he is spending wearing himself out with Shirzad is much needed. Thanks, Shirzad. You are the good man that the rest of us younger men aspire to be.

And for me missing my wrestling family this year, well, at least I have Shirzad... my friend, my coach, my mentor. And now, so does Dakota.

Brian Preece: As Daniel and Dakota wait for wrestling to start in Connecticut, in Utah we are up and going. There are some COVID-19 protocols to follow on crowd size and tournaments are limited to 224 competitors, or basically, no tournament can have more than 16 wrestlers per weight for the 14 weight classes. The five matches a day rule is still enforced so some adaptations in brackets have had to be done. I recently ran a girl's tournament where we had the semi-final losers drop down to battle for third and fourth. Wrestlers that lost in the first round or quarter-finals could battle back for fifth place. That way we can still have large one-day tournaments and stay within the rules.

I was also on the committee for our all-star dual. We moved it back a week because COVID-19 forced our season back basically two weeks. Our athletes have to do weekly COVID-19 testing and that actually impacted our event as several wrestlers tested positive. We had to scramble to make last-minute replacements. But we still had a good event and made some adaptations to limit crowd size and the number of competitors. Instead of a traditional format we have done recently where everything started at 7:00 p.m., we spread the event over three sessions starting at 3:30 p.m. in the afternoon. We also actually expanded the number of matches, especially the girl's matches, to 16 bouts versus maybe just three.

This year our state association sanctioned girls wrestling, and we have over 600 girls wrestling in Utah. The quality of these girls is also improving. Our top girl Sage Mortimer actually didn't compete in the all-star dual because she was invited to wrestle in the Jordan Burroughs-David Taylor undercard matches in Omaha, Nebraska. Sage is still the first girl to All-American at the USA Wrestling nationals in Fargo against the boys, and surprisingly for a state with a very conservative political and cultural culture, girls wrestling is doing well in the Beehive State. And we just might see Sage, though still in high school, at the 2020 Olympic Trials.

Our state's biggest invitational tournament, the Rockwell Rumble, decided to go on but was going to be bigger than what our state association allowed. So the event organizer, my friend Cole Kelley, decided not to sanction with our state high school association, but with USA Wrestling. And the event was going to run on a Sunday/Monday on the Dr. Martin Luther King Jr. holiday weekend. No team scores will be kept and athletes must register by club, not high school.

Since the Church of Jesus Christ of Latter-day Saints (also known as the Mormon Church) has such a powerful impact on our state and it generally frowns upon its followers competing on Sunday, the schedule did cut down on the number of Utah participants. But the out-of-state entrants have skyrocketed and made up more than half of the field of wrestlers. States like California, Nevada, Oregon, and Washington have canceled their seasons due to COVID-19, so the kids in these states, starved for opportunities, have flocked to this event. And it also should be said, we have had a lot of move-ins to Utah, regardless of the sport, and these athletes are making huge impacts for their teams.

I think this presents a unique opportunity for my friend Cole to really expand this tournament going forward, so it perhaps rivals the big tournaments like the Doc Buchanan and the Reno Tournament of Champions out west in both quality and quantity of participants. Put on a good event, and many of these out-of-state athletes and teams could return, and with a full complement of Utah wrestlers next year when the event goes back to a Friday-Saturday format, the tournament could have well over 1000 wrestlers and 100 teams. I was asked by Cole to help with the seeding this year to help make sure the best wrestlers meet in the finals and medal, which again could help sell the event as one that is well run and fair to its participants regardless of the state in which they compete.

The state tournaments will be one-day events, so the modified bracket I described earlier will have to be used. This has upset some wrestling purists, but it is what it is. Coaches, wrestlers, and parents are just glad for the opportunity and Utah remains one of the few states where athletics is taking place pretty close to what people might call "normal fashion." COVID-19 can still take out individual athletes and even teams like it did in some of our fall sports playoffs, but the games and matches are going on. In wrestling, skin infections often disqualify wrestlers at state and state qualifying meets, but COVID-19 could do the same and have huge impacts on the sport heading into the final stages of the season.

I know people could look at Utah and think we are out of our minds to try to have high school athletics. Our infection rates in the Beehive State have been among the highest in our nation during these winter months. I take COVID-19 seriously and fully support some of the precautions we are doing in the state like the mask mandate for businesses, and of course some of the precautions we are taking in our schools and with interscholastic athletics. Yet, at the same time, I think our young people deserve as much of a normal life as possible. I think a balance can be found between following safety protocols to help combat the spread of COVID-19, while at the same time not just denying our youth everything that could bring them both joy and the important life lessons that come from extracurricular involvement.

My own son Zach graduated in 2020 and lost some opportunities. I fully accept why schools across the nation shut down and extracurriculars generally got shut down in the spring and summer months because we just didn't know what we were dealing with. But as we have learned more about the Coronavirus itself, and how losing these things have impacted our youth, I have to say I generally support the approach Utah has taken in this regard. But I will also say this, if we get to the point where our hospitals are overrun, we might have to change   our   approach. My personal politics is one that the virus is not a hoax and is something we should take seriously. But we also should not live in complete fear and deny our children opportunities to do the things they enjoy. I also think the young people that are missing most of the opportunities are the less affluent. The people with wealth from some of these states that aren't having competitions can afford to travel to Utah to compete in the Rockwell Rumble or other big youth tournaments like the Salt Lake Slam or the Beehive Brawl, the latter I just worked at as an announcer. COVID-19 has exposed many inequities in our society, and the opportunity to engage in youth sports is just one of those examples. The rich get to play, the poor lose out.

Ultimately, we have to be flexible in our plans. And so while high school wrestling in Utah has made some adaptations that purists might not like, the chance for our young people to wrestle outweigh some of these inconveniences. I know Dakota missed his sophomore season due to injury, I would hate to see COVID-19 wipe out his junior year as well.

CHAPTER FOURTEEN

NON-CONTACT WRESTLING IS

AN OXYMORON

Dan Blanchard: According to what we've been hearing from the Connecticut Interscholastic Athletic Conference (CIAC), the governing body for secondary school athletics, and the Department of Public Health (DPH), this Tuesday, January 19th, is supposed to be the start of winter sports. Unfortunately, the alternative spring football season will no longer occur because winter sports got pushed back so far due to the pandemic. However, the CIAC has given the go-ahead for winter sports with some caveats.

The CIAC categorized the risk of each sport and laid out guidelines. The only low-risk sport is swimming. That can go on as normal with crowd-control measures. Basketball, ice hockey, gymnastics, and indoor track are moderate-risk. These moderate-risk sports obviously need to limit spectators. All participants have to wear a mask at all times. And they will have an abbreviated season. Wrestling, competitive cheer, and competitive dance are high-risk. They will be limited to small group conditioning and non-contact skill-building activities for the entire season.

Non-contact wrestling... which also means no matches for the entire season... I don't know about you, but that just doesn't feel like wrestling to me. Dakota and I anxiously await to find out what non-contact wrestling is. What does that look like?

Well, January 19th is upon us now, and wrestling isn't. There is no wrestling season taking place. So, I guess Dakota and I now know what non-contact wrestling looks like. It looks like nothing... nothing at all. Dakota's junior year of wrestling is lost...

Dakota began his wrestling journey his freshman year of high school with the goal of becoming a state champ. I supported his mission because I knew the extreme demands of this sport would forge his character into a good man who becomes a leader and is brave enough to take on difficult things. I knew the sport of wrestling would make my son a good man someday, even if he did not know that yet.

But... so much has been taken away from Dakota. He had a fantastic freshman year where he came out for the team as a freshman who had never wrestled before. He was a natural. He was extremely athletic, super flexible, and a quick study. He made the varsity wrestling team as just a freshman. And ended up with a winning record that year. However, about two-thirds of the way through the season, he injured his knee.

After his freshman year wrestling season, Dakota participated in off-season wrestling. He continued to grow by leaps and bounds. Dakota looked like he was on track to be a state champ wrestler for his senior season. However, he also kept having intermittent knee problems during the spring and summertime of his freshman year. These knee problems sidelined him entirely during the fall of his sophomore year. He ended up needing surgery in the fall. His meniscus was torn in three spots and was folding over. Dakota missed his entire sophomore high school wrestling season due to that surgery.

I kept telling him to not worry about it. He was still young, and he'd have the off-season in the spring and summer to make up for it. Then came COVID-19. And the State of Connecticut shut down all sports. Even though Dakota's knee appeared to finally be better, there is no longer any spring, summer, or fall wrestling in our state in 2020.

With trepidation, we kept looking toward November 30th for the start of his junior high school season. When it didn't happen, we turned our gaze toward January 19th, which is now here, but without wrestling. They are now telling us it is doubtful that there will be any off-season wrestling either in the spring and maybe even summer.

It really is a very short journey from one's high school freshman year to senior year. I never knew the trip could really be this short. I thought Dakota was right on track and had plenty of time to learn all that he needed to learn to be a state champ and wrestle in Fargo at the Junior Olympics, as well. Now, it looks like life is once again proving me wrong. Very wrong. I'm not blaming anyone for this. Life throws a lot of curveballs. However, so many opportunities have been taken away from Dakota to learn what is necessary to become a state champ. Now, I know that door isn't closed yet. But, it certainly isn't as wide open as it once was during his freshman year.

To go from freshman year to jump right to his senior year and be a state champ is a very big ask. I don't know if Dakota will be a state champ or not. And I feel really bad for him if he doesn't reach his goal. But, as his father and coach, I've always known that this wrestling journey has never really been about the gold medal. It's always been about the development of a good man. And that part of this journey is still on track. While Dakota may not be dealing with learning how to suck it up when you're tired and down. He certainly is learning that life throws many curveballs. And you have to always keep your head up and adapt, improvise, and overcome. And sometimes you have to go to Plan B. And sometimes, not getting your dreams gives you your destiny of what you're really supposed to be doing with your life.

Dakota is still on track to become a good man. Only time will tell about the gold medal on top of the podium. And... there's always college wrestling if that's a road that Dakota decides on his own that he wants to go down...

Brian Preece: My only wish is that states like Connecticut would study what Utah has done with its high school athletics. It's not like there aren't restrictions, but the games and meets are going on. In wrestling, tournaments are limited to no more than 224 competitors, and often, depending on local health departments, crowd sizes are limited or even prohibited. I think most people have accepted this and are just grateful that competition is going on. Athletes are also tested weekly and obviously held out if they test positive. Sometimes parents have to watch their children wrestle through some livestream service or through Trackcast. I just wish again that Connecticut would look at how Utah is doing things and see what is happening to infection rates in the state and in the schools and then make decisions on the best data available.

At the youth tournament I helped with, we limited wrestlers to one coach. One Mom that wanted to be on the floor to video or whatever went off on us but most people again understood the rule and were grateful their child could compete. We also did these on deck squares where the wrestlers stood inside them with their one coach with masks on until they took the mat. All wrestlers and coaches had to enter one way and exit the other, and to get on the floor they had to check in. We had plenty of coaches and athletes alike that tried to circumvent that but it generally worked. But we, as tournament managers, thought maybe this was the way to go for future tournaments, COVID-19 or not. Fans in the stands could see, the tables weren't overrun with parents, coaches, and wrestlers standing around. It was just a quieter, less chaotic environment. I'm not sure I want to totally return to "normal" in some things because, in some ways, these COVID-19 protocols have caused event organizers to clean up their events and get spectators off the floor. And just how many adults do we need to coach a wrestler matside anyhow?

I am fearful that Dakota will lose his junior season after losing his sophomore season. And Daniel spoke well about how this loss of mat time will hinder his dreams of taking state. But Daniel is also correct in saying there are more important things in life than being a state champion. Being a good man, a good citizen, a good husband, and a good father are more important than standing on top of a podium with a medal around your neck.

In our first book, I did speak of a young man that I coached that lost his sophomore and junior seasons due to a neck injury. I definitely want to mention him by name in this book as Travis Ayoso was one of the best athletes and people I was ever blessed to coach. He wanted to wrestle so badly. Finally, the doctors cleared him midway through what was his senior season. So basically he had five weeks to wrestle and get prepared for state. He actually won our region (league) and placed in state. He didn't take state and obviously missing the majority of his high school career hindered that greatly. But Travis is a good man raising his children to be good people. I feel confident that Dakota is on the right path and has a great mentor in Daniel.

CHAPTER FIFTEEN

DAKOTA LOSES ANOTHER SEASON

Dan Blanchard: This is the weekend of February 20th. It's supposed to be the weekend of the Class L State Championships here in Connecticut. My son, Dakota, was supposed to have had a great season racking up many wins. I also pictured him placing in the States at 145 pounds just as his Dad had done at his age. But… it wasn't meant to be. The COVID-19 pandemic canceled our wrestling season and took away Dakota's chance to wrestle this year.

Last year at this time, we were trying to get Dakota's knee healthy enough for him to salvage his lost sophomore season. We were hoping he'd wrestle in the States and win some matches there to offset not wrestling during the year.

Dakota battled hard in the States his freshman year at his Dad's old freshmen weight class of 126-pounds. And he did pretty well by taking the fifth-seeded wrestler deep into the third period before losing the match. His sophomore year, at 132-pounds, I thought Dakota could place in the States for sure. But, it didn't happen because his knee surgery kept him sidelined the entire season, regardless of how much physical therapy he did.

This year, even with Dakota missing his whole sophomore year, I thought he'd have a really good season and do very well in the States. I thought for sure he'd do well enough to qualify for the State Open tournament. There was a small piece of me that was wishfully hoping he'd win the Class L State Championship as a junior at the 145-pound class. I had won States my junior year at 145-pounds in the Class LL State Championship. Like father like son. Another title would have been so cool. But... it didn't happen. Life throws curveballs at us more often than it doesn't.

In some ways, Dakota's arc of wrestling has been very similar to mine. Dakota didn't wrestle until high school, like me. He wrestled at 126-pounds like me, his freshman year, even though he is much taller than I was at that age. He even made the varsity team as just a freshman and had a winning record and a good showing in States. Just like I did at his age. And if his team had awarded the "Rookie of the Year" trophy, I think he had an excellent chance of winning it as I had done all those years ago.

Dakota's sophomore year, he had grown some more and now was a lot taller than me. But somehow, he still made weight for the 132-pound weight class. The same weight class I had wrestled as a sophomore. In my sophomore year, I ran into some issues with being sick and missed a few matches. Dakota had knee surgery and missed the whole season of competition.

However, he never missed a practice, just like I didn't when I broke my finger my freshman year. My sophomore year, I placed in States, and we all thought Dakota would too if we could just get his knee back, but as I said earlier, it didn't happen. It just wasn't meant to be his sophomore year.

In my junior year, I jumped up two weight classes to 145 pounds and won the Class LL States. I knew in my heart, and from lots of coaching experience for many years that it was a very big ask for Dakota to do the same. But I also knew there was a slimmer of hope that he could indeed do it. This year, Dakota's junior year, he weighed in at 145-pounds, and his knee seemed to be fully back. It was a long shot, but there was a chance for him to do something really big this season... However, COVID-19 moved in... and we all know what happened next... No more wrestling in Connecticut.

This year we had no States. No wrestling season. And there won't be any spring off-season wrestling either here in this part of Southern New England. Now the question becomes, will there be any wrestling this summer and/or next fall to get Dakota ready for his senior year of man's oldest sport... and his last chance to reach his goal of being a high school wrestling state champ...

I sure hope so, but if, for some reason, things don't work out and Dakota doesn't reach his goal of becoming a high school state champion, well, it's not the end of the world. I'd love to see him do it. But it's also okay if he doesn't do it, as long as he gives it his all. And if he gives it his all, and it doesn't work out. I will still be proud of him because I will have known by then that wrestling has helped him become a good young man.

Brian Preece: While there was no wrestling season in Connecticut, in Utah the last of six boys' classification and three girl classification state tournaments wrapped up on February 20.

There were restrictions, as coaches had to wear masks, only parents could attend (or each athlete was given two tickets), and for the first time since the late 1980s, some of the classification tournaments were housed in high school gymnasiums. Also, the state tournaments were one-day affairs and a new bracket type was used so that the five-match-a-day rule was not violated. Basically, wrestlers that lost in the semifinals would wrestle for third place, and the best a wrestler could do if they lost in the first or second rounds was fifth place. Some of the qualifying divisional tournaments were held without spectators and were actually held over two days with special exemption because 32-wrestler brackets were needed to be used. These were some of the adaptations done in Utah so our boy and girl wrestlers could compete. And of course, athletes and coaches were tested for COVID-19 on a regular basis.

Some athletes and coaches tested positive so they were quarantined, but by the divisional tournaments, I heard of no COVID-19 (or even skin infection) disqualifications. It's not that it didn't happen, I just didn't hear of any. And the tournaments went off without a hitch. The 6A tournament even had a "ring" announcer that really spiced up the event. So, though high school gyms were used for the 5A and 6A classifications, there were still a lot of the bells and whistles of recent state tournaments. Auxiliary gyms were used for some of the tournaments, and I noticed at the 6A boys state tournament that the school cafeteria was used for team seating so athletes could better socially distance. If competitors were beaten and knocked out of the tournament, it was suggested that they should leave, which some did.

At the 6A girls tournament, one auxiliary gym was used not for competition, but for housing teams who could watch the tournament on TV as it was Trackcasted. So there were some clever adaptations taken to help with socially distancing and so forth. Still, one prominent coach did get a bad case of COVID-19, which I guess got into his heart, and he missed the state tournament. And some athletes that did get COVID-19 did get flu-like symptoms. So yes, young, healthy athletes could get pretty sick, but none, to the best of my knowledge, had to be hospitalized.

No doubt the differences in political climates have led Connecticut and Utah to take different approaches. But I think there is the reality of how and when the virus hit each state the hardest that has impacted this as well. Connecticut is adjacent to New York, which got hammered by the virus early on. In Utah, there were very few cases in the spring as compared to Connecticut and other states on the east or west coast. But Utah did shut down its schools and spring sports. But since there were generally few cases and deaths, many people were upset.

The Utah cases stayed relatively low in the summer. In fact, the death rate of Utah is comparatively lower than most states. There are many theories for this. People cite how Utahns are more outdoorsy and active, certainly younger than most populations of other states, and the healthier lifestyles that many in Utah have that come from being members of the Church of Jesus Christ of Latter-Day Saints where the faithful abstain from smoking and drinking alcohol, all could contribute to a better situation in the Beehive State. And as of February 20, 2021, Utah actually has had over 80,000 more cases than Connecticut, but Connecticut has had five times the deaths. So bottom line, how the virus has hit each state, and when the virus hit each state, I think has definitely shaped the psyche of their people and certainly the approach of policymakers. Bottom line, Utah is way more open than Connecticut across the board.

It has definitely been interesting to see, say on CNN, how they are talking about the "opening of the schools" across the country and the plan for that, while schools in Utah have generally been opened since August. There have been some adaptations, certainly more students are doing online and there have even been school closures for a few days as cases in a school hit a certain threshold. And the Salt Lake City School District was the odd district out doing just online school for the first semester. But political pressure has led them to open up for the second semester. Utah cases did spike hard in mid-November, and winter sports did shut down for two weeks delaying the start of the wrestling season. As cases got higher, there was some nervousness that high school athletics would be canceled, or seasons would be shut down for lengthy periods, but none of that happened at the macro-level. Sometimes dual meets, or games in basketball, had to be canceled, but there were no widespread shutdowns.

Utah did get some move-ins from out-of-state but the state athletic association said only students that made documented "full family moves" would be able to participate in sports. So there were no athletes able to live with "Uncle Johnny' or in the basement of the assistant coach. But in 6A, three move-ins made the finals and two took state. And in 4A, Uintah, where my father once coached and won nine state titles, returned to the top of the standings for the first time in 21 years. But they had two-move-ins that placed first and third in state, and if you take away their points, they place second in state. But it should be said that one of the move-ins did have strong family ties with the community. And a few other move-ins in the other classifications did place in these state competitions. But again, my intention isn't to get too political, but parents want their children to have opportunities, even if they have to pack up and leave their own communities for Utah. And generally, the athletes that were coming to Utah were elite level.

I know Colorado started up their wrestling season after January, and it's ending in late February. I have a grandnephew that is pretty tough. He would be a shoo-in to qualify for state under normal conditions, but in Colorado, they are only letting the top two wrestlers from their leagues go to state versus four in normal years. And there are no crowds allowed, except for senior night when they do allow parents to attend for that. But quite frankly, I'm glad he is getting an opportunity because I was worried, like Dakota, he would lose his season and he is a senior. I wonder if state associations from Colorado to Connecticut were studying what has happened in Utah with our schools being opened and athletics going on generally in a somewhat normal fashion.

And lastly, Utah had 384 girls compete in their state tournaments. But the reality, COVID-19 did hurt girls' participation in Utah a bit, and it hurt participation overall. And in Salt Lake City School District where they have three high schools, all online, only 11 boy wrestlers qualified for state, and overall participation was at an all-time low. One coach said the obvious, "it's really hard to recruit and communicate with athletes over a zoom meeting." So the strong programs got stronger and the weak programs suffered. It will be interesting to see what happens going forward. As for Dakota and Daniel, my heart aches for them losing another season.

CHAPTER SIXTEEN

FATHERS AND SONS CREATING MEMORIES

Dan Blanchard: Well, wrestling season in Connecticut has come and gone, and there aren't any post-season tournaments. The New England's would have taken place last weekend. This is such an exciting tournament. I was hoping Dakota would have gotten to experience it this year, but it didn't happen.

There had been some on-going rumors in Connecticut that they would push wrestling to the spring and maybe even take it outside in a much abbreviated season. But those ideas were scratched too because the spring sports had lost their seasons last year because of COVID-19. They didn't want short spring sports seasons this year because of winter sports, which hadn't been canceled in the previous year, pushing into their time and space this year.

Regarding the other states around us that make up New England, well, New Hampshire was the only state that allowed wrestling this year. Massachusetts and Rhode Island have moved their wrestling to the spring season. And Maine and Vermont, like Connecticut, canceled their season.

New York and New Jersey aren't part of New England, but they are indeed part of the northeast wrestling family. Both are allowing wrestling to commence. I believe they both will have very short seasons to try to limit their impact on spring sports.

In addition, I have recently been told that the Nationals are back on in Virginia Beach this spring. I just bumped into one of my old buddies, a Connecticut wrestling coach, at one of my daughter's soccer games. And he told me he was taking a group of wrestlers down and asked if I was going with Dakota. I hesitated. Hey, I would love to take Dakota down there, but he hasn't really been training for it, and I don't want him to get hurt or sick. Hey, we're still in a pandemic.

When my buddy saw my hesitation, he said, "Hey, I know you're crazy busy. Just give me Dakota, and I'll take him down." I was moved by his kindness and generosity. But I still said no because I want more shots in arms, and I want Dakota to have been on the mat more before I put him in that kind of competition. And nothing is open up here in Connecticut for him to get that sort of mat time. Also, I'm not sure that I'm comfortable with kids and their families coming from all over the country who I have no idea of what they've been doing or what their beliefs are in taking some standard precautions during this pandemic. I don't like not sending Dakota. But I would like it even less if he got sick, especially when we could have had a little more patience for more shots to get into some more arms. And then maybe hit up a few tournaments this summer instead.

Now, I know not all parents out there will agree with me on this one, especially if they are diehard wrestlers who feel that they have to be back on that mat. I know many people don't fully believe that this pandemic is as dangerous as the news has been saying. But, hey, this is America. Parents get a lot of freedom to follow their own conscience and do what they feel is best for their own children. So, for the people around our country who are wrestling, I say, "Good for you. I wish we were too. I wish you continued success and health" And for those who are refraining from wrestling, I say, "Good for you, too. Do what you think is right. Perhaps you really are better safe than sorry."

So, here is some good news in what I think I may be able to do for my son in a state that is still shut down when it comes to wrestling. I have a stimulus check coming my way in the next few weeks. I'm hoping to use some of that money to pay some bills that have piled up on me. In addition, I'm also hoping to put some of that money back into our economy by buying a 10 X 10 home wrestling mat for my unfinished basement for Dakota.

As you may recall from previous writings, Dakota, who had never wrestled before high school, had a fantastic freshman year. Unfortunately, his sophomore year was robbed by a knee surgery right before the season started. Then his junior year was taken as well by the pandemic. He only has one more year to do what he wants to do for his high school wrestling career, and he needs some time on the mat to do it. If I can get a home wrestling mat, I can give him some of that time on the mat back several times a week through drilling with me. It would also be some great father-son time together. And give him a fighting chance during these crazy times to have the kind of senior year he wants to have.

Wish us luck… We're going to need it…

Next, something really cool just happened. While driving in my car, Dakota and I talked about wrestling, and he mentioned how so much of wrestling is in one's head. He asked me what he could do to help him mentally with wrestling. I told him that I have spoken often and written books and articles on winning and putting yourself in the right state of mind to win. However, I really wanted him to go to the source that inspired me so many years ago and changed my thinking that has helped me become more successful.

When we got home, I rummaged through my basement and found one of my favorite books of all time. It is a book called, *Awaken the Giant Within* by Anthony Robbins. I read this book as a very young man in the early 1990s. It opened my eyes to the psychology of winning. The book is 30 years old, and it still has my original pen scribbled notes in it. It's amazing that I still have it, found it, and it is still in good shape. I was pumped to share the genesis of my positive and peak performance way of thinking and behaving with my son. I just pray he gets as much out of it as I did. If he does, he'll be in a great position to train his brain and control his thoughts on that wrestling mat and to continue to do so long after wrestling is over in other arenas of his life.

Finally, Dakota and I have bumped into the college wrestling coaches lately. They told him that they thought he was a pretty good wrestler. And then demanded that he gets nothing but A's from now on in his schooling because he needs very good grades to open doors for college.

Now I feel like we're really making some great progress in molding my son Dakota into a good young man who trains his body, mind, and character through the sport of wrestling and doing hard things.

Brian Preece: As I pointed out in previous chapters, unlike Connecticut, Utah had a wrestling season. In fact, only two weeks of practice time and almost three weeks of competition time were lost. Instead of our wrestlers getting 40-60 matches for their season, most got in the 20-40 range, depending on how things went. Weekly COVID-19 testing went on, and some teams and individual wrestlers did test positive and lost competitive opportunities. But in the end, the season went on. It was also the first season in Utah for sanctioned girls wrestling. So in some senses, the Utah high school wrestling season in 2020-21 was highly successful.

Daniel's desire to get a small wrestling mat to work out with Dakota did remind me of some times with my Dad. My wife Heidi got me a really cool Christmas present this year. She bought some service where old VHS tapes could be put on DVD and the cloud. One of the converted VHS tapes was when we were at our church playing basketball. My cousins from the Denver, Colorado area were visiting, and they love hoops. We must have just bought our video camera, and my Mom and/or my Aunt Carol filmed us. My Dad and my Mom's brother Emery, who was also my Dad's fraternity brother in college, along with their children, played some pick-up basketball. Both my Dad and Emery played high school basketball, and both were reportedly good players. My cousins and my sister all played high school basketball. And though I wrestled in high school, I wanted to show that I actually had some game too.

We played some half-court 2-on-2, with the winning teams staying on. My Dad paired up with Emery. I paired up with my cousin Clay, the youngest of Emery's children, who was about 13 years-old. Walt, Emery's oldest son, who was a year younger than me as I was 17 at the time, paired up with my little brother Scott, who was 10 years-old. My sister paired up with Shane, Emery's middle child, and the two of them were age 14. The idea was to have teams that were competitive with each other. It was just fun to watch this video and see my Dad as an athlete. My father passed away in 1997, at age 55. I am 12 years older now than he was in that video. That was surreal to think about when I watched this video, and I admit, I both laughed and cried as it brought back a flood of great memories.

I would like to think that all of my siblings and my cousins have lived very successful lives. I could see in the video the traits that drove them as athletes and coaches for my own siblings. But I also saw some of the old parenting styles where parents didn't intervene every time there was a problem. If we called a foul and a member of the other team disagreed, we had to work it out. No parents came to the rescue. And when my cousin Walt knocked my sister to the floor on a hard foul, neither Mom nor Dad intervened. In a proverbial sense, my sister dusted herself off and went back into battle with the boys. Years later, it only made sense that she would become one of the most successful volleyball coaches in our state's history. She has won six state titles at two different schools and is currently closing in on her 500th career victory.

We were all competitors and good athletes. My cousin Walt would play college football, and all my cousins would play basketball on their high school teams. But probably the most competitive person out there was my younger brother Scott. And when I watched his video, I was seeing a future state champion wrestler, a 3-sport athlete in high school, and a guy in his later life who would run marathons and do triathlons. That competitive fire was there at an early age.

I also saw in that video two great fathers. They were different in their styles. My Uncle Emery was quiet, steady, and kind, while my father was boisterous, always the life of the party. But I'm very grateful that I have had both in my life. And also very thankful for my Mom and Aunt Carol as well.

I feel bad that Dakota has lost his second season of wrestling. That has been very difficult, I'm sure, for both father and son. I hope though, with that 10 X 10 wrestling mat, that the two will create some cherished memories as father and son. And maybe Dakota can earn some good takedowns on his Dad like I scored some hoops on my father.

Finally, once again, as I said in the closure of our first book, I can't wait to see what Dakota does next year...

ABOUT THE AUTHORS

Dan Blanchard: Bestselling and Award-Winning, Author, Speaker, and Educator. TV Host. Two-time Junior Olympian Wrestler and two-time Junior Olympian Wrestling Coach who grew up as a student-athlete. However, Dan admits that as a youth he was more of an athlete than a student. Dan has now successfully completed fourteen years of college and has earned seven degrees. He teaches Special Education and Social Studies in Connecticut's largest inner-city high school where he was chosen by the AFT-CT as the face and voice of educational reform and is now on the speaking circuit for them. Dan was with the team that put forth Connecticut's new Social Studies Frameworks and is also a member of the Special Education Advisory Board to the Connecticut State Department of Education. In addition, Dan is a Teacher Consultant for the University of Connecticut's Writing Project. Finally, Dan is a double veteran of the Army and the Air Force. Find out more about Dan and his other books: www.DanBlanchard.net.

Brian Preece: Brian can't really remember a time when he wasn't involved in the sport of wrestling. His father Dennis, a Hall of Fame wrestling coach from the State of Utah, introduced Brian to the sport at a young age in the early 1970s. As a competitor, Brian won a state freestyle championship and was a 2-time region (league) champion, as well as a 2-time state placer in high school. He wrestled one year at Brigham Young University before embarking on a teaching and coaching career that spanned over 30 years. As a coach, he was recognized as the 2006 Utah Coach of the Year by the National Wrestling Coaches Association. Besides coaching, Brian also was an official, event organizer, and an early benefactor to the Utah Valley University wrestling program. But he is perhaps best known in Utah wrestling circles for the media coverage and historical perspective he has brought to the sport for parts of five decades. By joining forces with author Daniel Blanchard, the two hope to bring a fresh perspective of the father-son dynamic that is truly unique to the sport of wrestling. Brian currently resides in Mapleton, Utah, and with his wife, Heidi, and are the proud parents of two adult children (Lizzy age 21, and Zach age 19).